ACADEMIC
VOCABULARY

VOWEL SOUNDS		CONSONANT SOUNDS	
Symbol	Examples	Symbol	Examples
a	act, bat	b	back, cab
ā	day, age	ch	cheap, match, picture
âr	air, dare	d	door, head
ä	father, star	f	fan, leaf, phone
e	edge, ten	g	give, dog
ē	speed, money	h	her, behave
ə*	ago, system, easily, compete, focus	j	just, page
		k	king, bake, car
ēr	dear, pier	l	leaf, roll
i	fit, is	m	my, home
ī	sky, bite	n	note, rain
o	not, wasp	ng	sing, bank
ō	nose, over	p	put, stop
ô	law, order	r	red, far
oi	noise, enjoy	s	say, pass
o͞o	true, boot	sh	ship, push
oo	put, look	t	to, let
yo͞o	cute, united	th	thin, with
ou	loud, cow	TH	THat, baTHe
u	fun, up	v	value, live
ûr	learn, urge, butter, word	w	want, away
		y	yes, onion
		z	zoo, maze, rise
		zh	pleasure, vision

*This symbol, the *schwa,* represents the sound of unaccented vowels. It sounds like "uh."

© 2005 Pearson Education, Inc.

DATE DUE

MAY 1 3 2009	
SEP 1 1 2012	

ACADEMIC VOCABULARY

Academic Words

Second Edition

Amy E. Olsen

Cuesta College

PEARSON
Longman

New York   San Francisco   Boston
London   Toronto   Sydney   Tokyo   Singapore   Madrid
Mexico City   Munich   Paris   Cape Town   Hong Kong   Montreal

Vice President and Editor-in-Chief: Joseph Terry
Senior Acquisitions Editor: Susan Kunchandy
Senior Marketing Manager: Melanie Craig
Senior Supplements Editor: Donna Campion
Production Manager: Donna DeBenedictis
Project Coordination, Text Design, and Electronic Page Makeup: Elm Street Publishing Services, Inc.
Cover Designer/Manager: John Callahan
Cover Photos (from top to bottom): Topham/The Image Works; Photodisc Blue/Getty Images; Georges Seurat (French 1859–1891), *A Sunday on La Grande Jatte* (detail), 1884–86. Oil on canvas, 207.6 x 308 cm. Helen Bartlett Memorial Collection, The Art Institute of Chicago. 1926.224. Photograph © 2001, The Art Institute of Chicago. All Rights Reserved; John Lamb/Stone/Getty Images.
Art Studios: Elm Street Publishing Services, Inc.; Gil Adams
Photo Researcher: Photosearch, Inc.
Senior Manufacturing Buyer: Alfred C. Dorsey
Printer and Binder: Quebecor World Dubuque
Cover Printer: Phoenix Color Corporation

Photo credits: **p. 5 (L, R):** Everett Collection, Inc.; **p. 10 (T):** Topham/The Image Works; **p. 10 (M, B):** Getty Images; **p. 19 (T):** Burke/Triolo Productions/Brand X Pictures/Getty Images; **p. 19 (B):** Michael Newman/Photo Edit; **p. 20 (T):** Getty Images; **p. 20 (B):** Mark Richards/Photo Edit; **p. 28:** Antonio M. Rosario/Photographer's Choice/Getty Images; **p. 31 (T):** Eric Meola/The Image Bank/Getty Images; **p. 31 (B):** SPL/Photo Researchers, Inc.; **p. 36 (T):** Charles Gupton/Stone/Getty Images; **p. 36 (B):** Ilene Perlman/Stock, Boston, LLC; **p. 39:** David Young-Wolff/Photo Edit; **p. 41:** Joe Sohm/The Image Works; **p. 45 (T):** Robert Daly/Stone/Getty Images; **p. 45 (M):** Time Life Pictures/Getty Images; **p. 45 (B):** Bettman/Corbis; **p. 49:** Davis Barber/Photo Edit; **p. 53:** Emma Lee/Life File/Photodisc Green/Getty Images; **p. 56 (R):** Syracuse Newspapers/Al Campanie/The Image Works; **p. 56 (TL):** Chris Ladd/Taxi/Getty Images; **p. 56 (BL):** Spike Mafford/Photodisc Green/Getty Images; **p. 61 (T):** John Elk/Stock, Boston, LLC; **p. 61 (B):** Carlos Navajas/The Image Bank/Getty Images; **p. 66 (T):** David Hosking/Photo Researchers, Inc.; **p. 66 (B):** DPA/The Image Works; **p. 70:** Topham/The Image Works; **p. 71:** David Young-Wolff/Photo Edit; **p. 79:** John Lamb/Stone/Getty Images; **p. 82 (T):** Syndicated Features Limited/The Image Works; **p. 82 (B):** Getty Images; **p. 86 (T):** Bill Aron/Photo Edit; **p. 86 (B):** Digital Vision/Getty Images; **p. 92:** Jeff Greenberg/Photo Edit; **p. 95 (T):** Vic Bider/Photo Edit; **p. 95 (B):** Jeff Greenberg/Photo Edit; **p. 96 (T):** David Weintraub/Photo Researchers, Inc.; **p. 96 (M):** John Eastcott & Yva Momatiuk/The Image Works; **p. 96 (B):** John Serrao/Photo Researchers, Inc.; **p. 104:** Michael Melford/National Geographic Society/Getty Images; **p. 107 (L):** Alan & Linda Detrick/Photo Researchers, Inc.; **p. 107 (R):** Color Day/Getty Images; **p. 112 (T):** Terry Vine/Stock/Getty Images; **p. 112 (B):** David Young-Wolff/Photo Edit; **p. 114:** Photodisc Blue/Getty Images; **p. 117 (L):** Getty Images; **p. 117 (R):** AKG/Photo Researchers, Inc.; **p. 122:** Robert Brenner/Photo Edit; **p. 129:** Corey Rich/Lonely Planet Images/Getty Images; **p. 132 (T):** Will & Deni McIntyre/Photo Researchers, Inc.; **p. 132 (B):** Joseph Drivas Photography; **p. 135:** Jeff Greenberg/Photo Edit; **p. 137:** Rapho Agence/Photo Researchers, Inc.; **p. 142 (L):** Elizabeth Crews/The Image Works; **p. 142 (R):** Frank Siteman/Stock, Boston, LLC; **p. 145:** Getty Images; **p. 155:** Jeff Greenberg/The Image Works

Please visit us at **http://www.ablongman.com**

ISBN 0-321-14259-4

2 3 4 5 6 7 8 9 10—QWD—07 06 05 04

DEDICATION

To Matthew and Keri
Future vocabulary leaders and people who know how to make
learning and life fun!

—AMY E. OLSEN

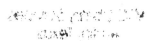

CONTENTS

PREFACE

Because students benefit greatly from increased word power, the study of vocabulary should be enjoyable. Unfortunately, vocabulary workbooks often lose sight of this goal. To help make the study of vocabulary an exciting and enjoyable part of college study, I have written *Academic Vocabulary*.

The goal of this book—the third in a three-book interactive vocabulary series—is to make the study of vocabulary fun through a variety of thematic readings, interactive exercises, and self-tests. As a casual glimpse through the book will indicate, these activities involve writing, personal experience, art, and many other formats. The goal of these activities is simple: to utilize individual learning styles in order to help students learn new words in a large number of contexts.

Underlying the text's strong visual appeal is a strong underlying philosophy: an essential part of learning vocabulary is repeated exposure to a word. *Academic Vocabulary* provides nine exposures to each word.

▌▌ CONTENT OVERVIEW

Each chapter follows a specific and consistent format.

- **Thematic Reading:** Because most vocabulary is acquired through reading, each chapter begins with a thematic reading that introduces ten vocabulary words in context. These readings come in a variety of formats including journal entries, newsletters, and interviews. The goal is to show that new words may be encountered anywhere. Rather than simply presenting a word list with definitions, the readings give students the opportunity to discover the meanings of these new words via context clues.

  The themes for *Academic Vocabulary* were chosen from disciplines that most students will encounter at some point in their college careers. In choosing the words, I've been guided by three factors: (1) relation to the chapter theme, (2) use in textbooks, novels, magazines, and newspapers, and (3) my own experiences in teaching reading and writing.

- **Predicting:** The second page of each chapter contains a Predicting activity that gives students the chance to figure out the meaning of each vocabulary word before looking at its definition. The Predicting section helps students learn the value of context clues in determining a word's meaning. While the text does offer information on dictionary use, I strongly advocate the use of context clues as one of the most active methods of vocabulary development.

- **Word List:** Following the Predicting activity is a list of the words with a pronunciation guide, the part of speech, and a brief definition for each. I wrote these definitions with the idea of keeping them simple and nontechnical. Some vocabulary texts provide complicated dictionary definitions that include words students do not know; I've tried to make the definitions as friendly and as useful as possible.

- **Self-tests:** Following the Word List are three Self-tests in various formats. With these tests, students can monitor their comprehension. The tests include text and sentence completion, true/false situations, matching, and analogies. Some tests employ context clue strategies using synonyms and antonyms and general meaning. Critical thinking skills are an important part of each test. (Answers to the Self-tests appear in the Instructor's Manual.)

- **Interactive Exercise:** Following the Self-tests is an Interactive Exercise that asks students to begin actively using the vocabulary words. The activity may include writing, making lists, or answering questions. The Interactive Exercises give students the chance to really think about the meanings of the words, and, more importantly, they encourage students to begin using the words actively.

ADDITIONAL FEATURES

In addition to the thematic vocabulary chapters, *Academic Vocabulary* includes a Getting Started chapter, three Word Parts chapters, three Review chapters, an Analogies Appendix, and instructions for making flash cards with templates provided. A pronunciation key appears on the inside front cover, and an alphabetical list of all the vocabulary words (with page references) is included on the inside back cover.

- **Getting Started:** *Academic Vocabulary* begins with an introductory chapter to familiarize students with some of the tools of vocabulary acquisition. The "Parts of Speech" section gives sample words and sentences for the eight parts of speech. "Using the Dictionary" dissects a sample dictionary entry and provides exercises for using guide words.
- **Word Parts:** The three Word Parts chapters introduce prefixes, roots, and suffixes used throughout this book. Students learn the meanings of these forms, and sample words illustrate the forms. Self-tests in each Word Parts chapter give students the opportunity to practice using the word parts.
- **Review Chapters:** Three Review chapters focus on the preceding nine chapters. They divide the words into different activity groups and test students' cumulative knowledge. The words appear in artistic, dramatic, written, test, and puzzle formats. These repeated and varied exposures increase the likelihood that the students will remember the words, not just for one chapter or test but for life.
- **Analogies Appendix:** The appendix explains how analogies work and provides two sample exercises. The exercises illustrate common relationships used in analogies.
- **Flash Cards:** At the back of the book is a Flash Card section that teaches students how to create and use their own flash cards. There are also flash card templates to get the students started. Students can use their cards for self-study, and instructors may want to use the cards for the supplemental activities and games found in the Instructor's Manual.
- **Pronunciation Key:** On the inside front cover is a pronunciation key to help students understand the pronunciation symbols used in this text. The inside front cover also offers some additional guidelines on pronunciation issues.

FEATURES NEW TO THIS EDITION

- **Refined In-Chapter Organization:** The Interactive Exercises are now the last exercise provided in each chapter since these exercises are more likely to provide a greater benefit to students once they have completed all of the practice exercises in the chapter.
- **More Exercises:** An additional practice exercise (Self-test) is now included in each chapter. This extra exercise gives students even further practice to learn each vocabulary word.
- **New Predicting Exercise Format:** Students will now write out the definition from a choice of five definitions instead of picking from A to C. Writing the definition will help students better remember the meaning of a word. The Predicting directions also ask students to cover the Word List below to make the Predicting section more meaningful.
- **Hints:** A Hint box has been added to every other chapter. The hints deal with improving vocabulary, reading, and study skills. The hints are brief and practical, and students will be able to make use of them in many of their college courses.
- **Updated CD-ROM:** The CD-ROM that accompanies *Academic Vocabulary* has been updated to include more effective and relevant exercises.

THE TEACHING AND LEARNING PACKAGE

Each component of the teaching and learning package for *Academic Vocabulary* has been carefully crafted to maximize the main text's value.

- **Instructor's Manual and Test Bank (0-321-05501-2):** The Instructor's Manual and Test Bank, which is almost as long as the main text, includes options for additional classroom activities such as collaborative exercises and games. The Collaborative Exercises usually ask students to share their work on the Interactive Exercises in small groups or with the whole class. These exercises give students the opportunity to practice using the words with other people. Some of the games are individual; others are full-class activities. Some games have winners, and some are just for fun. The games may involve acting, drawing, or writing.

  The Test Bank, formatted for easy copying, includes three tests for each chapter as well as Mastery Tests to accompany the Review chapters and full-book Mastery Tests that can be used as final exams.

- *Academic Vocabulary* **CD-ROM:** In this computer age many students enjoy learning via computers. Available with this text is the *Academic Vocabulary* CD-ROM, which features additional exercises and tests that provide for even more interaction between the students and the words. The CD-ROM has an audio component that allows students to hear each chapter's thematic reading and the pronunciation of each word as often as they choose. Students are often reluctant to use the new words they learn because they aren't sure how to pronounce them. The pronunciation guides in each chapter do help address this fear, but actually hearing the words spoken will give the students greater confidence in using the words. Contact your Longman sales representative to order the student text packaged with the CD-ROM.

- **The Dictionary Deal:** Two dictionaries can be shrink-wrapped with this text at a nominal fee. *The New American Webster Handy College Dictionary* is a paperback reference text with more than 100,000 entries. *Merriam-Webster's Collegiate Dictionary,* tenth edition, is a hardback reference book with a citation file of more than 14.5 million examples of English words drawn from actual use. For more information on how to obtain a shrink-wrapped dictionary with the text, please contact your Longman sales representative.

- **MySkillsLab (www.myskillslab.com):** This site opens the door to a world of dynamic multimedia resources and gives students all the multimedia solutions they'll need to develop reading and writing skills in one easy-to-use place. Students can gain access to the Longman Vocabulary Website for additional vocabulary-related resources as well as access to grammar tools, reading software, and research engines. Please contact your Longman sales representative for further information.

ACKNOWLEDGMENTS

I want to thank the following reviewers for their helpful suggestions as the book took shape for both the first and second editions: Kathy Beggs, Pikes Peak Community College; Diane Bosco, Suffolk County Community College; Janet Curtis, Fullerton College; Carol E. Dietrick, Miami-Dade Community College; Patrice Haydell, Delgado Community College; Miriam A. Kinard, Trident Technical College; Belinda Klau, Imperial Valley College; John M. Kopec, Boston University; Maggi Miller, Austin Community College; Susan Sandmeier, Columbia Basin College; Kerry Segel, Saginaw Valley State University; Kathleen Sneddon, University of Nebraska, Lincoln; Shirley Wachtel, Middlesex County College; and Carolyn J. Wilkie, Indiana University of Pennsylvania.

Thanks also to Susan Kunchandy, Basic Skills Senior Acquisitions Editor, for her assistance in organizing this edition. Commendations go to the Supplement and Marketing sections of Longman for their efforts on different aspects of the book. Many thanks to those at Elm Street Publishing Services for making this series visually appealing. I am grateful to several colleagues across California for our significant discussions on reading and writing at diverse conferences and other gatherings. A huge (belated) thank you to Karl for his support of my teaching and writing and for our long, comforting conversations at the end of a tough week. Finally, I offer my deepest appreciation to family and friends who have been encouraging over the years. A special thank you to my mom and dad for all their love and support.

I am proud to present the second edition of *Academic Vocabulary,* a book that continues to make learning vocabulary fun and meaningful.

—AMY E. OLSEN

TO THE STUDENT

This book is designed to make learning vocabulary fun. You will increase the benefits of this book if you keep a few points in mind.

1. **Interact with the words.** Each chapter contains seven exposures to a word, and your instructor may introduce one or two additional activities. If you're careful in your reading and thorough in doing the activities for each chapter, learning the words will be fun and easy.

2. **Appreciate the importance of words.** The words for the readings were picked from textbooks in a variety of academic disciplines, magazines, newspapers, novels, and lists of words likely to appear on standardized tests (such as the SAT and GRE). These are words you will encounter in the classroom and in everyday life. Learning these words will help you be a more informed citizen and will make your academic life much richer. Even if you don't currently have an interest in one of the readings, keep an open mind: the words may appear in the article you read in tomorrow's newspaper or on an exam in one of next semester's classes. The readings also come in different formats as a reminder that you can learn new vocabulary anywhere, from a newsletter to a memo.

3. **Find your preferred learning style.** This book aims to provide exercises for all types of learners—visual, aural, and interpersonal. But only you can say which learning style works best for you. See which activities (drawings, acting, matching, completing stories) you like most, and replicate those activities when they aren't part of a chapter.

4. **Remember that learning is fun.** Don't make a chore out of learning new words, or any other new skill for that matter. If you enjoy what you're doing, you're more likely to welcome the information and to retain it.

Enjoy your journey through *Academic Vocabulary!*

—AMY E. OLSEN

Getting Started

There are eight parts of speech. A word's part of speech is based on how the word is used in a sentence. Words can, therefore, be more than one part of speech. For an example, note how the word *punch* is used below.

nouns: (n.) name a person, place, or thing

> EXAMPLES: Ms. Lopez, New Orleans, lamp, warmth
>
> *Ms. Lopez* enjoyed her *trip* to *New Orleans* where she bought a beautiful *lamp*. The *warmth* of the *sun* filled *Claire* with *happiness*. I drank five *cups* of the orange *punch*.

pronouns: (pron.) take the place of a noun

> EXAMPLES: I, me, you, she, he, it, her, we, they, my, which, that, anybody, everybody
>
> *Everybody* liked the music at the party. *It* was the kind that made people want to dance. *They* bought a new car, *which* hurt their bank account.

verbs: (v.) express an action or state of being

> EXAMPLES: enjoy, run, think, read, dance, am, is, are, was, were
>
> Lily *read* an interesting book yesterday. I *am* tired. He *is* an excellent student. She *punched* the bully.

adjectives: (adj.) modify (describe or explain) a noun or pronoun

> EXAMPLES: pretty, old, two, expensive, red, small
>
> The *old* car was covered with *red* paint on *one* side. The *two* women met for lunch at an *expensive* restaurant. The *punch* bowl was empty soon after Uncle Al got to the party.

adverbs: (adv.) modify a verb, an adjective, or another adverb

> EXAMPLES: very, shortly, first, too, soon, quickly, finally, furthermore, however
>
> We will meet *shortly* after one o'clock. The *very* pretty dress sold *quickly*. I liked her; *however,* there was something strange about her.

prepositions: (prep.) placed before a noun or pronoun to create a phrase that relates to other parts of the sentence

> EXAMPLES: after, around, at, before, by, from, in, into, of, off, on, through, to, up, with
>
> He told me to be *at* his house *in* the afternoon. You must go *through* all the steps to do the job.

conjunctions: (conj.) join words or other sentence elements and show a relationship between the connected items

> EXAMPLES: and, but, or, nor, for, so, yet, after, although, because, if, since, than, when
>
> I went to the movies, *and* I went to dinner on Tuesday. I will not go to the party this weekend *because* I have to study. I don't want to hear your reasons *or* excuses.

interjections: (interj.) show surprise or emotion

> EXAMPLES: oh, hey, wow, ah, ouch
>
> *Oh,* I forgot to do my homework! *Wow,* I got an A on the test!

▬▬▮▮ USING THE DICTIONARY

There will be times when you need to use a dictionary for one of its many features; becoming familiar with dictionary **entries** will make using a dictionary more enjoyable. The words in a dictionary are arranged alphabetically. The words on a given page are signaled by **guide words** at the top of the page. If the word you are looking for comes alphabetically between these two words then your word is on that page.

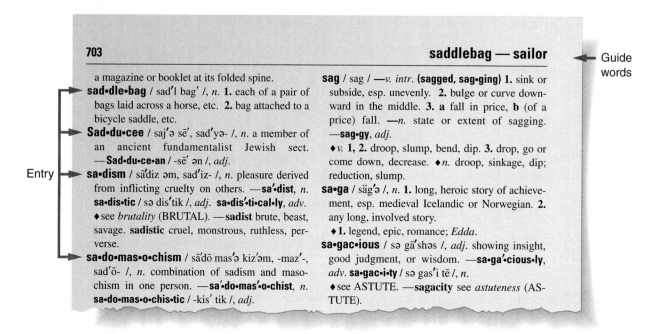

SOURCE: *The Oxford Dictionary and Thesaurus, American Edition,* edited by Frank Abate, © 1996 by Oxford University Press, Inc. Used by permission of Oxford University Press, Inc.

Most dictionaries contain the following information in an entry:

- The **pronunciation**—symbols show how a word should be spoken, including how the word is divided into syllables and where the stress should be placed on a word. The Pronunciation Key for this book is located on the inside front cover. The key shows the symbols used to indicate the sound of a word. Every dictionary has a pronunciation method and a pronunciation key or guide is usually found in the front pages, with a partial key at the bottom of each page. The differences in the pronunciation systems used by dictionaries are usually slight.
- The **part of speech**—usually abbreviated, such as *n.* for noun, *v.* for verb, and *adj.* for adjective. A key to these abbreviations and others is usually found in the front of the dictionary.
- The **definition**—usually the most common meaning is listed first followed by other meanings.
- An **example of the word in a sentence**—the sentence is usually in italics and follows each meaning.
- **Synonyms** and **antonyms**—*synonyms* are words with similar meanings, and *antonyms* are words with opposite meanings. (You should also consider owning a **thesaurus**, a book that lists synonyms and antonyms.)
- The **etymology**—the history of a word, usually including the language(s) it came from.
- The **spelling of different forms** of the word—these forms may include unusual plurals and verb tenses (especially irregular forms).

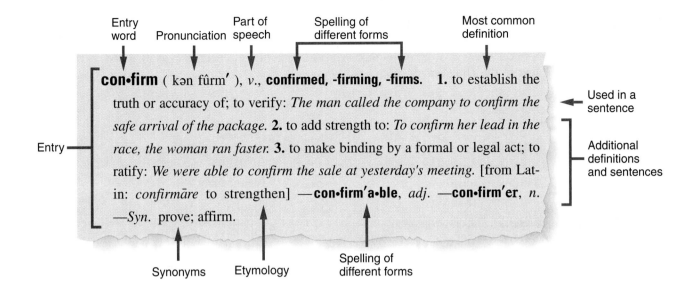

When choosing a dictionary, take the time to look at different dictionaries and see what appeals to you. Dictionaries come in several sizes and are made for different purposes. First read some of the entries and see if the definitions make sense to you. See which of the features above are used in the dictionary. Is it important to you to be able to study the etymology of a word? Would you like sample sentences? Some dictionaries have illustrations in the margins. Decide if that is a feature you would use. Check to see if the print is large enough for you to read easily.

Decide on how you will use this dictionary. Do you want a paperback dictionary to put in your backpack? Or is this going to be the dictionary for your desk and a large hardback version would be the better choice? Several disciplines have specialized dictionaries with meanings that apply to those fields, such as law or medicine. There are also bilingual dictionaries, such as French/English or Spanish/English that can be helpful for school or travel. Take time in picking out your dictionary because a good dictionary will be a companion for years to come. A few dictionaries to consider are *Webster's College Dictionary, The American Heritage Dictionary, The Random House College Dictionary,* and *The Oxford Dictionary.*

In general, when you are reading try to use context clues, the words around the word you don't know, to first figure out the meaning of a word, but if you are still in doubt don't hesitate to refer to a dictionary for the exact definition. Don't forget that dictionaries also contain more than definitions and are an essential reference source for any student.

▌▌▌ USING GUIDE WORDS

Use the sample guide words to determine on which page each of the ten words will be found. Write the page number next to the entry word.

Page	Guide Words
157	bone/boo
159	boot/born
435	endemic/endorse
654	humanist/humongous
655	humor/hunter
975	pamphlet/pandemonium
976	pander/pant
1480	velvet/venom

EXAMPLE: <u>654</u> humdinger

_____ 1. pang

_____ 2. Panama

_____ 3. bonnet

_____ 4. vengeance

_____ 5. endive

_____ 6. hunk

_____ 7. booth

_____ 8. pansy

_____ 9. humanoid

_____ 10. hummus

▌▌▌ ENTRY IDENTIFICATION

Label the parts of the following entry.

① **②** **③** **④** **⑤**

a•ble (ā′ bəl) *adj.* **a•bler, a•blest.** 1. having the necessary power, skill, or qualifications to do something: *She was able to read music.* **⑥**

⑦ 2. having or showing unusual talent, intelligence, skill, or knowledge: *Washington was an able leader.* [1275–1325; ME < MF < L **⑧** *habilis* easy to handle, adaptable=*hab(ēre)* to have, hold + *ilis* –ile] Syn. apt, talented.

⑨

1. _____

2. _____

3. _____

4. _____

5. _____

6. _____

7. _____

8. _____

9. _____

The Back of the Box

Box 1

"**Hailed** as a masterpiece, *Wild Strawberries* is a film that deserves its reputation."
—*Sunday Examiner*

Ingmar Bergman's
Wild Strawberries

5

Wild Strawberries is a feast of a film. The **cinematography** brilliantly uses black-and-white contrasts to show the disturbed thoughts of an old man as he faces death, and an honorary degree. The **surreal** dream sequences take us into his past and into his **disconcerted** mind. Clocks without hands and an examination room with strange questions are among the unusual experiences Dr. Borg faces. The **juxtapositions** of old age and youth force us, as well as the doctor, to examine life and our actions.

10

15

Starring
Victor Sjostrom, Bibi Andersson, Ingrid Thulin, Gunnar Bjornstand, and Max Von Sydow

20

Directed by
Ingmar Bergman
Screenplay by
Ingmar Bergman
Produced by
Allan Ekelund
25
Photography by
Gunnar Fischer
Costumes by
Millie Strom
30
Edited by
Oscar Rosander
Music by
Erik Nordgren

In Swedish with English subtitles 1959 B&W 90 minutes

Box 2

Alfred Hitchcock's
Psycho

"For the **connoisseur** of suspense, Hitchcock's films are a must, and *Psycho* is among the best."
—Paula Cole, *Find Me at the Movies*

5

"*Psycho* is the **epitome** of the suspense movie. It holds all the thrills an audience expects from the unexpected."
—*The New Mexico Tribune*

Alfred Hitchcock is the master of the suspense **genre**. Hitchcock was **attuned** to the darker sides of human nature and was able to convey the fears and desires of lust and greed in fascinating images. In the shower scene, for example, Hitchcock uses **montage** to create the suspense. Through careful editing, he brings the tension to the audience without ever showing the plunging knife.

10

15

Starring
Anthony Perkins, Vera Miles, John Gavin
Costarring Martin Balsam, John McIntire,
and
Janet Leigh

20

Directed by Alfred Hitchcock
Screenplay by Joseph Stefano

This film has been modified from its original version to fit your TV.

25

Cover the Word List below as you do the Predicting exercise. For each set, write the definition on the line next to the word to which it belongs. If you are unsure, return to the reading on page 5, and underline any context clues you find. After you've made your predictions, uncover the Word List and check your answers. Place a checkmark in the boxes next to the words whose definitions you missed. These are the words you'll want to study closely.

SET ONE

fantastic   approved enthusiastically   disturbed   the art of motion picture photography the act of placing close together

❑   1.   **hailed** (box 1, line 1) _____

❑   2.   **cinematography** (box 1, line 7) _____

❑   3.   **surreal** (box 1, line 10) _____

❑   4.   **disconcerted** (box 1, line 11) _____

❑   5.   **juxtaposition** (box 1, line 14) _____

SET TWO

a style   a film editing technique   a person who can judge the best in a field a thing that is typical of a group   adjusted

❑   6.   **connoisseur** (box 2, line 3) _____

❑   7.   **epitome** (box 2, line 6) _____

❑   8.   **genre** (box 2, line 9) _____

❑   9.   **attuned** (box 2, line 10) _____

❑ 10.   **montage** (box 2, line 13) _____

▊▎▊ WORD LIST

attune
[ə tōōn', ə tyōōn']
v. to adjust; to bring into harmony

cinematography
[sin' ə mə tog' rə fē]
n. the art or technique of motion picture photography

connoisseur
[kon' ə sûr', -soor']
n. a person who can judge the best in an art or other field

disconcerted
[dis' kən sûrt' əd]
adj. disturbed; disordered; confused

epitome
[i pit' ə mē]
n. a person or thing that is typical of a whole group; embodiment

genre
[zhän' rə]
n. a class of artistic work (movie, book, etc.) that has a particular form, content, or technique; a style

hail
[hāl]
v. 1. to approve enthusiastically
2. to cheer; to welcome; to call out to

juxtaposition
[juk' stə pə zish' ən]
n. an act of placing close together, especially for comparison or contrast

montage
[mon täzh']
n. 1. a film editing technique that presents images next to each other to convey an action, idea, or feeling
2. the combining of various elements to form a whole or single image

surreal
[sə rē' əl, rēl']
adj. unreal; fantastic; having the quality of a dream

▮▮▮▮ SELF-TESTS

1 Circle the correct meaning of each vocabulary word.

1. hail: welcome ignore
2. connoisseur: unsure of quality judge of the best
3. genre: a style an exception
4. montage: separate combining to form a whole
5. attune: adjust clash
6. epitome: embodiment singular
7. disconcerted: clear confused
8. surreal: fantastic factual
9. cinematography: art of writing art of motion picture photography
10. juxtaposition: putting far apart placing close together

2 These comments are overheard as people file out of the multiplex movie theater. Match each sentence to the word it best fits. Use each word once.

VOCABULARY LIST

genre	surreal	attuned	disconcerted	juxtaposition
montage	hail	epitome	connoisseur	cinematography

1. "The desert scenes were beautifully filmed. They really showed the richness of color in the sand and the sunsets." _____
2. "That was a great film! It's going to be the year's best movie!" _____
3. "Even though it was so strange, I liked it when everyone started flying around and speaking that strange language." _____
4. "I had to get used to the relaxed pace of the movie, but once I did, I really enjoyed the film." _____
5. "I am an expert on horror movies, and I can tell you this was not one of the director's best efforts." _____
6. "It really disturbed me when the movie began jumping back and forth between the past and the present." _____
7. "Next time we are staying home and renting Westerns; those are my kinds of movies." _____
8. "It was interesting how the blonde woman was standing next to old cars in so many scenes. I think the director was trying to make a point about stereotypes in America." _____
9. "That film represents everything I dislike about musicals, especially having people break into a song every ten minutes." _____
10. "I liked the part where the director put the various shots of prison life together to show the boredom of the prisoners." _____

3 Finish the sentences. Use each word once.

1. My father is a chocolate _____; he will eat nothing but the finest European choco-lates.

2. My favorite movie _____ is the musical, but my husband prefers horror movies.

3. The _____ of scenes on a quiet beach with the freeway traffic really showed that the character needed to escape the pressures of the big city.

4. The vivid colors used in the film caused me to pay attention to the _____ over the other elements such as music and plot.

5. By being _____ to the latest trends, some producers can create a movie that capital-izes on a fad such as skateboarding or disco dancing.

6. It is easy to become _____ in today's multiplex theaters; I went to get popcorn and couldn't find my way back without asking an usher for directions.

7. The newspaper reviewer loved the concert; she _____ it as the best performance in the symphony's twenty-year history.

8. In *Battleship Potemkin,* Eisenstein's skillful editing of scenes showing the poor treatment of the sailors creates a powerful _____ of the men's discontent.

9. To me the _____ of evil is shown in the scene where the man throws the child off the roof.

10. It was a(n) _____ experience when I woke up in a hotel room and thought I was in my own bedroom.

HINT

Flash Cards

Flash cards are a great way to study vocabulary. Turn to the "Create Your Own Flash Cards" section at the end of this book (page 161) for suggestions on ways to make and use flash cards. Remember to carry your flash cards with you and study for at least a few minutes each day. Also ask classmates, friends, and family members to quiz you using the flash cards. There are a few templates to get you started at the end of this book. Make copies of them before you fill them all out if you want to use them for all the chapters in this book.

Answer the following questions.

1. What is your favorite movie genre? _____

2. What might happen in a surreal dream?

   _____

3. What would look unusual juxtaposed next to a piece of fruit?

   _____

4. What are you a connoisseur of or what would you like to be a connoisseur of?

   _____

5. What can you do to be better attuned to the feelings of others?

   _____

   _____

6. Which movie star do you think is the epitome of style? _____

7. What movie do you think has beautiful cinematography?

   _____

8. What could happen in a movie to make you feel disconcerted?

   _____

   _____

9. What would you hail as a great achievement of humankind?

   _____

   _____

10. If you were to create a montage showing the first day of kindergarten, what are three images you would use?

    _____   _____   _____

New Sounds

Welcome to tonight's event! The Rolling Rock Show is designed to share fifty years of rock history in one night with over twenty performers on stage playing the songs you love.

5   The history of rock 'n' roll has been filled with turmoil. In the 1950s the **bravura** of early rock performers such as Elvis Presley with his swiveling hips startled many conservative Americans. They referred to rock 'n' roll as a **cacophony** and **censured** its being played on the radio or
10 sold in record stores. But the "noise" could not be stopped or the movement quieted. Over the next few years rock 'n' roll continued to break down the **decorum** of the young as crowds of women chased after the Beatles, screamed through their songs, and fainted at their concerts. During
15 the 1960s, the young **clamored** for even more energetic music. The **execution** of rock music continued to change as rock venues grew. Performers learned to **modulate** their voices and performances depending on whether they were singing in front of thousands at a concert like Woodstock or
20 before an intimate group at a folk café. Performers like Jimi Hendrix and Janis Joplin showed how instruments and voices could be used in dynamic ways.

The complaints against rock music seemed barely **audible** by the mid-1970s when punk rock and the Sex
25 Pistols broke the peace. High energy was again vital to the music scene, and poor **acoustics**, found in many of the small halls punk bands first played in, hardly seemed to matter to audiences that spent the night pogoing and slam dancing. Music continued to evolve, and the 1980s and 90s
30 embraced a variety of styles including new wave, hip-hop, and rap. For many performers today, it isn't unusual for their **repertoire** to include a classic song (like "Heatwave") from one of the 60s girl groups to a heavy-metal inspired number.

35 Tonight's concert brings artists together from the 1950s to the present to perform songs from some of their most popular albums as well as works by other rock greats. Enjoy the fun, the flair, and the flavors of rock 'n' roll!

■■■■ PREDICTING

Cover the Word List below as you do the Predicting exercise. For each set, write the definition on the line next to the word to which it belongs. If you are unsure, return to the reading on page 10, and underline any context clues you find. After you've made your predictions, uncover the Word List and check your answers. Place a checkmark in the boxes next to the words whose definitions you missed. These are the words you'll want to study closely.

SET ONE

a harsh sound   dignified conduct   a display of daring   stated noisily
criticized in a harsh manner

❑ 1. **bravura** (line 6) _____

❑ 2. **cacophony** (line 9) _____

❑ 3. **censured** (line 9) _____

❑ 4. **decorum** (line 12) _____

❑ 5. **clamored** (line 15) _____

SET TWO

all the works an artist can perform   a style of performance   capable of being heard
to adjust   the features of a room that determine the quality of sounds in it

❑ 6. **execution** (line 16) _____

❑ 7. **modulate** (line 17) _____

❑ 8. **audible** (line 24) _____

❑ 9. **acoustics** (line 26) _____

❑ 10. **repertoire** (line 32) _____

■■■■ WORD LIST

acoustics
[ə k$\overline{oo}$′ stiks]

n. the features of a room or auditorium that determine the quality of the sounds in it

audible
[ô′ də bəl]

adj. capable of being heard; loud enough to hear

bravura
[brə vyoor′ ə]

n. a display of daring; a brilliant performance

cacophony
[kə kof′ ə nē]

n. a harsh, discordant sound

censure
[sen′ shər]

v. to criticize in a harsh manner

n. 1. a strong expression of disapproval
2. an official reprimand

clamor
[klam′ ər]

v. to state noisily

n. a loud uproar; a loud and continued noise

decorum
[di kôr′ əm, kōr′]

n. dignified conduct or appearance

execution
[ek′ si kyo͞o′ shən)]

n. 1. a style of performance; technical skill, as in music
2. the act of doing or performing
3. the use of capital punishment

modulate
[moj′ ə lāt′]

v. to alter (the voice) according to circum-stances; to adjust

repertoire
[rep′ ər twär′, -twôr′, rep′ ə-]

n. 1. all the works that a performer is prepared to present
2. the skills used in a particular occupation

1 Circle the word that best completes each sentence.

1. The (cacophony, acoustics) in the concert hall were so good I could hear the characters when they whispered.

2. The performers (execution, repertoire) surprised me. Not only could he sing and dance, but he could do magic and tell jokes.

3. The soft voice on the phone was scarcely (audible, modulate), but I thought it was my three-year-old niece who answered.

4. The gymnast's (clamor, execution) on the balance beam was flawless.

5. As the clapping increased or decreased, the candidate knew just how to (modulate, censure) her voice for the best effect.

6. The artist's (bravura, repertoire) was amazing; we couldn't believe he had dared to put the dictator's head on the body of a pig.

7. The executive board voted to (modulate, censure) the treasurer for failing to keep receipts for all of his expenses last year.

8. The crowd (clamored, censured) for an encore, and the band obliged by playing three more songs.

9. The (decorum, execution) at the luncheon was disturbed when the waiter dropped a tray of sandwiches in the lap of noble Lady Windermere, thus causing the other women to giggle.

10. Someone had played with my radio, and I awoke to a (decorum, cacophony) of static, which upset my morning.

2 For each set, write the letter of the most logical analogy. See the Analogies Appendix on page 159 for instructions and practice.

SET ONE

_____	1. modulate : voice ::	a. decorum : rudeness
_____	2. lecture : classroom ::	b. sprain : ankle
_____	3. bravura : boldness ::	c. execution : boring
_____	4. early : late ::	d. shy : modest
_____	5. taste : salty ::	e. censure : Senate meeting

SET TWO

_____	6. audible : silent ::	f. difficult : hard
_____	7. fire : burns ::	g. brave : cowardly
_____	8. water : pool ::	h. a car crash : cacophony
_____	9. clamor : noise ::	i. book : chapters
_____	10. pianist : repertoire ::	j. acoustics : auditorium

3 Finish the stories using the vocabulary words. Use each word once.

SET ONE

VOCABULARY LIST

acoustics	audible	repertoire	clamor	cacophony

I was disappointed by the concert. First, the (1)_____ were so bad I couldn't hear the music.
Then the management fiddled with the sound system, and the (2) cacophony_____ that emitted from
the speakers caused the audience to cover its ears. Finally, even when the music was
(3)_____ and not terrifying, we still weren't pleased. The new problem was the band's
(4)_____. It turned out they had only five original songs, and they kept playing them over
and over. The audience raised such a(n) (5)_____ about the poor quality of the whole
evening that the owners eventually gave us back our money.

SET TWO

VOCABULARY LIST

censure	modulate	execution	bravura	decorum

During rehearsals the director told the singer that she needed more (6)_____ in her performance. He told her that her (7)_____ did not fit her character. She was supposed to be a
crazy gypsy, and her dignified behavior did not fit the role. He emphasized that he did not mean to
(8) censure_____ her whole performance, just the second act where the audience needed to see and
feel the pain at her lover's betrayal. She needed to (9) modulate_____ her voice from a soft, sad beginning to an almost wild scream by the end. Her (10) execution_____ of the piece would help to estab-
lish her character and her actions later in the opera.

■ ■ ■ INTERACTIVE EXERCISE

Write your own program notes. Pick a type of music or a performer and let the audience know what to expect from the show. Include at least seven of the vocabulary words in your write-up.

Some styles of music to choose from:

Rock   Country & Western   Rap   Blues   Hip-Hop   Alternative

_____

_____

_____

_____

_____

_____

_____

_____

_____

_____

_____

_____

_____

_____

_____

_____

_____

_____

_____

_____

_____

_____

_____

_____

_____

3 Marketing

The High-in-the-Sky Ad Campaign

TALLORIN MARKETING

May 23, 2005

Quistex
964 Broad St.
Charleston, SC 29401

Dear Mr. Quist,

We have reviewed your company's history in regard to the advertising campaign you want to pursue. Though you have always been a **proponent** of new ideas, we do not feel that your plan is **feasible** at this time. While your generosity is **laudable**, your idea may be too much for the public to handle.

Your firm enjoys a **prestigious** place in American business. From its **inception** thirty years ago, your family has worked diligently to make Quistex one of the most trusted technology firms in the country. Your skills as an **entrepreneur** are highly admired by people in the business world. You have had amazing insight into when to develop technical innovations from computers to cell phones. You are also well respected for your **philanthropy**. Your donations of time and money to many good causes from art museums to hurricane victims have been a model for all humanity.

It is because of your excellent reputation that we would like to recommend some alterations to your marketing plan. While marketing always involves some **conjecture** as to what will interest the public, we feel that this idea may cause too much interest. Throwing dollar bills from an airplane into a crowded street may not be **conducive** to maintaining your reputation as a stable company. We feel an ad campaign that focuses more on your company's past performance will earn you more respect. Your idea would certainly attract notice, but again, we are uncertain whether it would be of the right kind. It is certainly your **prerogative** to continue with the "Raining Dollars" plan, but we hope that you will meet with our firm to discuss other options.

Sincerely,

Daniel Tallorin

Daniel Tallorin
CEO Tallorin Marketing

▌▌▌ PREDICTING

Cover the Word List below as you do the Predicting exercise. For each set, write the definition on the line next to the word to which it belongs. If you are unsure, return to the reading on page 15, and underline any context clues you find. After you've made your predictions, uncover the Word List and check your answers. Place a checkmark in the boxes next to the words whose definitions you missed. These are the words you'll want to study closely.

SET ONE

honored   an advocate   commendable   the act of beginning   possible

❑   1.   **proponent** (line 8) _____

❑   2.   **feasible** (line 8) _____

❑   3.   **laudable** (line 9) _____

❑   4.   **prestigious** (line 10) _____

❑   5.   **inception** (line 10) _____

SET TWO

a special right   benevolence   tending to assist   a conclusion made by guessing
one who assumes the risks of a business

❑   6.   **entrepreneur** (line 12) _____

❑   7.   **philanthropy** (line 14) _____

❑   8.   **conjecture** (line 17) _____

❑   9.   **conducive** (line 19) _____

❑   10.   **prerogative** (line 22) _____

▌▌▌ WORD LIST

conducive *adj.* tending to promote or to
[kən dōō′ siv] assist

conjecture *n.* a conclusion made by
[kən jek′ chər] guessing; a supposition
v. to arrive at by guessing

entrepreneur *n.* one who assumes the
[än′ trə prə nûr′] risks of a business or
enterprise

feasible *adj.* capable of being done;
[fe′ zə bəl] possible; suitable

inception *n.* the act of beginning
[in sep′ shən]

laudable *adj.* worthy of praise;
[lô′ də bəl] commendable

philanthropy *n.* general benevolence;
[fi lan′ thrə pē] an active effort to help
others

prerogative *n.* a special right, power,
[pri rog′ ə tiv] or privilege

prestigious *adj.* honored; having a
[pre stij′ əs, stē jəs] commanding position

proponent *n.* one who argues in
[prə pō′ nənt] favor of something; an
advocate

1 In each group, circle the word that does not have a connection to the other three words.

EXAMPLE: executive   manager   (worker)   entrepreneur

An executive, manager, and entrepreneur all have to be responsible for the risks of a business while a worker does not have to be involved in this aspect of a job.

1. advocate	attacker	proponent	defender
2. laudable	commendable	poor	praiseworthy
3. opening	beginning	inception	conclusion
4. impossible	suitable	attainable	feasible
5. conjecture	guess	supposition	certainty
6. generosity	benevolence	greed	philanthropy
7. laborer	investor	entrepreneur	businessperson
8. right	privilege	prerogative	powerless
9. honored	prestigious	noble	disgraced
10. helpful	worthless	conducive	useful

2 Finish the ad copy using the vocabulary words. Use each word once.

VOCABULARY LIST

entrepreneur	feasible	conjectures	prerogative	prestigious
philanthropy	inception	conducive	proponent	laudable

1. To impress your guests, nothing is more _____ than serving a Gobbler Turkey for Thanksgiving.

2. It's a woman's _____ to change her mind, but you won't once you try Derriere Jeans.

3. A warm cup of Matthew's Cocoa—nothing is more _____ to a relaxing evening.

4. Making learning educational and fun is a(n) _____ goal. We have achieved that goal at Kids Creative Software. Visit us today to see how.

5. Relive the days of the young _____ who set up the lemonade stand on hot summer days—drink a glass of Keep-It-Cool today.

6. Some of the best _____ starts at home: give yourself a subscription to the Natural History Museum.

7. You didn't think a trip to Europe was _____ this summer. Think again! Quest Travel has tours for as little as $75 a day with all meals included.

8. From its _____ two hundred years ago, Northernmost College has been an institution that helps you build a future.

9. Visit Smartalert.com for books on every subject. We've always been a(n) _____ of brighter minds.

10. Making _____ won't give you extra closet space or a gorgeous view. Come to Hillside Acres and experience our spectacular new homes.

3 Put yourself in the following situations, and match each situation to the word that applies.

SET ONE

_____ 1. You give one hundred dollars to cancer research.

_____ 2. At the City Council meeting, you argue in favor of preserving an open area as a park instead of building a shopping mall.

_____ 3. As guest of honor, you get to decide where to eat.

_____ 4. You work extra hard and get an A on your research paper.

_____ 5. You are seated at the head table at a banquet.

a. proponent

b. prestigious

c. laudable

d. philanthropy

e. prerogative

SET TWO

_____ 6. You study whether you can attend a meeting at 6 p.m. and still make it to the movies with a friend at 8 p.m., twenty miles away.

_____ 7. You are there when the student council decides to start a recycling program on campus.

_____ 8. You invest $150 in stocks, and by following the market, you end up with $1500 in one year.

_____ 9. You make guesses as to why your friends stop talking when you get near.

_____ 10. You take a warm bath to help you go to sleep.

f. inception

g. conjecture

h. conducive

i. feasible

j. entrepreneur

HINT

Context Clues

This book encourages the use of context clues to help find the meaning of a word. *Context* means the words surrounding a specific word that give clues to that specific word's meaning. When you encounter a word whose meaning you don't know, keep reading the passage, looking for clues to help you decipher the meaning. These clues might be in the same sentence as the unknown word or in a sentence that comes before or after the word. Look for these types of clues in the passage:

Synonyms—words that have a similar meaning to the unknown word

Antonyms—words that mean the opposite of the unknown word

Examples—a list of items that explain the unknown word

General meaning—the meaning of the sentence or passage as a whole that could clarify the meaning of the unknown word

You will not find a context clue every time you encounter a word you don't know, but being aware of context clues will help you determine the meaning of many new words and make reading more enjoyable.

INTERACTIVE EXERCISE

Come up with a product and write a sales pitch for it using at least seven of the vocabulary words. Be creative; think about the types of products likely to generate interest among your friends and family.

4 U.S. History

Challenges Faced

Before the United States became a country, immigration was a part of the American experience. Tired of being **persecuted** for their religious beliefs, the Pilgrims set sail from Plymouth, England, in 1620. They did not seek **martyrdom** by leaving England to settle in the New World, just the opportunity to freely practice their religion. The 101 passengers faced being **destitute** as they left in September with two months of rough seas before them and arrival in a rugged, barely charted land as winter approached. Still, like future immigrants, they felt the challenges were worth the rewards. They took animals and seed to start a new colony, and despite many hardships, they survived. A new country was set in motion, and settlers steadily continued arriving.

The nineteenth century was to see a period of mass migration. In 1846–47 the potato crop began to fail in Ireland and economic and political problems hit other European countries. Many Europeans saw America as a place for **autonomy**. There they believed they would be free to start their own businesses or farms and make their own religious and political decisions. Of course, many did not come without

ambivalence. It was difficult to leave family, friends, and a way of life they had known for years. It was political oppression, starvation, and a hope for a better future for themselves and their children that **induced** most people to come to America. Records show close to 24 million people arrived in the United States between 1880–1920. An immigration period of such **magnitude** has not been repeated in the United States.

Most immigrants have done their **utmost** to find a place in American society. Balancing a respect for their original country with their new homes has not always been easy. Maybe one of the hardest aspects has been **placating** the second and third generations who have not always understood the traditions of their parents and grandparents as they try to fit into American life. Many young people wonder why they must wear traditional clothing to celebrate holidays whose significance they don't really understand or why they must eat traditional foods when they want hamburgers and French fries. But these conflicts tend to resolve themselves with time as families **ascertain** how to combine customs from the old country with new ones from America to form a multicultural society, taking the best from the many lands that make up this New World.

■■■ PREDICTING

Cover the Word List below as you do the Predicting exercise. For each set, write the definition on the line next to the word to which it belongs. If you are unsure, return to the reading on page 20, and underline any context clues you find. After you've made your predictions, uncover the Word List and check your answers. Place a checkmark in the boxes next to the words whose definitions you missed. These are the words you'll want to study closely.

SET ONE

poor   having conflicting feelings   harassed   extreme suffering   independence

❑   1. **persecuted** (line 3) _____

❑   2. **martyrdom** (line 5) _____

❑   3. **destitute** (line 8) _____

❑   4. **autonomy** (line 18) _____

❑   5. **ambivalence** (line 20) _____

SET TWO

maximum   persuaded   calming   to find out definitely
greatness in significance, size, or rank

❑   6. **induced** (line 23) _____

❑   7. **magnitude** (line 25) _____

❑   8. **utmost** (line 27) _____

❑   9. **placating** (line 30) _____

❑ 10. **ascertain** (line 37) _____

■ ■■ WORD LIST

ambivalence
[am biv′ ə ləns]
n. having conflicting feelings, such as love and hate, about a person, object, or idea

ascertain
[as′ ər tān′]
v. to find out definitely; to learn with certainty

autonomy
[ô ton′ ə mē]
n. independence; the quality of being self-governing

destitute
[des′ tə tōōt′]
adj. devoid; poor; impoverished

induce
[in dōōs′]
v. 1. to persuade; to cause
2. to infer by inductive reasoning

magnitude
[mag′ ni tōōd′]
n. greatness in significance, size, or rank

martyrdom
[mär′ tər dəm]
n. 1. extreme suffering
2. the state of being a martyr (one who chooses death or makes a sacrifice rather than renounces religious faith or other belief)

persecute
[pûr′ sə kyōōt′]
v. to harass; to annoy continuously

placate
[plā′ kāt′, plak′ āt′]
v. to pacify; to calm

utmost
[ut′ mōst′]
n. the greatest amount or extent; maximum
adj. most extreme; of the greatest degree

1 Match the historical event to the rest of the sentence that completes the idea about the event's significance. You may need to do some research or consult a dictionary.

_____ 1. Landing on the moon

_____ 2. The Great Depression

_____ 3. The Civil War

_____ 4. The Declaration of Independence

_____ 5. The Salem witch trials

_____ 6. The discovery of gold at Sutter's Fort

_____ 7. The invention of the automobile

_____ 8. The Nineteenth Amendment

_____ 9. Prohibition

_____ 10. Building the Panama Canal

a. has created feelings of ambivalence depending on whether one is stuck in gridlock or enjoying the open road.

b. was fought because the South wanted autonomy.

c. led to martyrdom for those who would not admit to powers they didn't have or acts they didn't do.

d. left millions of people destitute.

e. was of the utmost concern because it took a ship two months to sail from the Pacific Ocean to the Atlantic Ocean during the Spanish-American War.

f. was a document of such magnitude that it led to the formation of a new country.

g. tried to placate concerns about the evils of drinking.

h. helped scientists ascertain what it is made of.

i. gave women the right to vote, ending years of persecution.

j. induced money-hungry people to head to California.

2 Use the vocabulary words to complete the following analogies. For instructions on how to complete analogies, see the Analogies Appendix on page 159.

VOCABULARY LIST

induce	persecute	destitute	martyrdom	ascertain
placate	utmost	magnitude	autonomy	ambivalence

1. soft : hard :: anger : _____
2. death : _____ :: packing : taking a trip
3. confused : disturbed :: _____ : poor
4. _____ : least :: fresh : stale
5. an interview : nervousness :: going away to college : _____
6. _____ : the truth :: catch : a train
7. performer : audience :: teenager : _____
8. hang : a painting :: _____ : labor
9. harass : _____ :: gentle : meek
10. feather : light :: The Great Barrier Reef : _____

3 Finish these historical headlines. Use each word once.

1. _____ of the American People Ends: Boston Tea Party Shows British What We Think of Taxation Without Representation (1773)

2. The _____ of the West Is "Amazing," Report Lewis and Clark (1806)

3. *President Lincoln Tries His _____ to Keep the Union Together (1860)*

4. _____ Indians Fight Back at Little Bighorn (1876)

5. San Francisco Earthquake Leaves Citizens _____ (1906)

6. Man Jumps to His Death! Suicide _____ by Stock Market Crash (1929)

7. Americans _____ Hitler's Goal as World Domination: U.S. Enters the War! (1941)

8. *Bra Burnings Said to Symbolize Women's _____ (1968)*

9. *The American People Won't Be _____ : President Nixon Must Go! (1974)*

10. Cell Phones and Computers—Greater Reliance on Technology Leads to _____ in Americans (2000)

▌▐▐ INTERACTIVE EXERCISE

Answer the following questions dealing with U.S. history.

1. Name two groups that have been persecuted. _____

   _____

2. Name two situations that have induced people to fight for changes in laws.

   _____   _____

3. The magnitude of the car's influence on American life continues to this day. Give three examples of its effects.

   _____   _____   _____

4. What are two kinds of autonomy people have fought for?

   _____   _____

5. Name an event that you think must have caused ambivalence in some people.

   _____

6. Name two events that have made people destitute.

   _____   _____

7. What are two possible actions the government can take to placate angry citizens?

   _____   _____

8. Which invention do you think has had the utmost influence on society? Why?

   _____

   _____

9. Name two ways you could ascertain which candidate you should vote for in the next mayoral election.

   _____   _____

10. What two beliefs might a person hold that could lead to martyrdom?

   _____   _____

5 Word Parts I

Look for words with these **prefixes**, **roots**, and/or **suffixes** as you work through this book. You may have already seen some of them, and you will see others in later chapters. Learning basic word parts can help you figure out the meanings of unfamiliar words.

prefix: a word part added to the beginning of a word that changes the meaning of the root
root: a word's basic part with its essential meaning
suffix: a word part added to the end of a word; indicates the part of speech

WORD PART	MEANING	EXAMPLES AND DEFINITIONS
Prefixes		
ambi-, amphi-	both, around	*ambivalence:* having conflicting feelings; feeling both ways *amphitheater:* a round structure with seats rising from an open space
auto-	self	*autonomy:* self-governing *autobiography:* writing about oneself
epi-	after, upon	*epilogue:* a speech after a play; material at the end of a book *epidermis:* the outermost layer of the skin; upon the surface
magni-	great, large	*magnitude:* greatness *magnify:* to make larger
post-	after, behind	*posterity:* future generations *postdoctoral:* pertaining to study done after receiving a doctorate
Roots		
-anthro-	human	*philanthropy:* a love of helping people *anthropology:* the study of humans
-duc-	to lead	*conducive:* leading toward *induce:* lead one to do
-ject-	to throw	*conjecture:* to throw out guesses *eject:* to throw out
-lev-	lift, light, rise	*alleviate:* to lighten; to reduce *elevator:* a device that lifts people

WORD PART	MEANING	EXAMPLES AND DEFINITIONS
-phil-	love	*philanthropy:* a love of helping people *philosophy:* a love of knowledge
-pos-, -pon-	to put, to place	*juxtaposition:* an act of placing close together *proponent:* one who puts one's point forward
-rog-	to ask	*prerogative:* a special right to ask for something *interrogate:* to ask questions
Suffixes		
-dom (makes a noun)	state or quality of	*martyrdom:* the state of suffering *freedom:* the quality of being free
-eur (makes a noun)	one who	*connoisseur:* a person who can judge the best in an art or other field *entrepreneur:* a person who assumes the risks of a business
-tude (makes a noun)	state or quality of	*magnitude:* the quality of being great *gratitude:* state of being thankful

▌▌▌ SELF-TESTS

1 Read each definition and choose the appropriate word. Use each word once. The meaning of the word part is underlined to help you make the connection. Refer to the Word Parts list if you need help.

VOCABULARY LIST

chauffeur	bibliophile	ambidextrous	automatic	levitate
postbellum	wisdom	misanthrope	conductor	deposit

1. capable of using <u>both hands</u>_____
2. occurring <u>after</u> a war_____
3. the person who <u>leads</u> the orchestra_____
4. <u>to put</u> money in the bank_____
5. running by <u>itself</u>_____
6. <u>one who</u> drives a car for a living_____
7. a person who <u>loves</u> books_____
8. someone who hates <u>humans</u>_____
9. <u>the quality of</u> being intelligent_____
10. to float or <u>lift</u> a person or thing_____

2 Finish the sentences with the meaning of each word part. Use each meaning once. The word part is underlined to help you make the connection.

VOCABULARY LIST

after	great	lead	threw	rise
love	put	ask	state	around

1. She received a <u>post</u>humous award: it was given to her the year _____ she died.
2. My free<u>dom</u> is important to me. It is a(n) _____ that I don't take for granted.
3. I moved the <u>lev</u>er to make the door _____.
4. The police inter<u>rog</u>ated the man for two hours; they had a lot of questions to _____.
5. My friends tried to se<u>duc</u>e me into going to the movies, but they couldn't _____ me astray; I stayed home and studied.
6. His answers were <u>ambi</u>guous: he kept dancing _____ my questions.
7. I trans<u>pos</u>ed the numbers on my check: I _____ the "1" before the "2" and ended up being nine dollars short.
8. Their house is <u>magni</u>ficent; everything about it is _____.
9. A phi<u>lat</u>elist has a(n) _____ of stamps.
10. I needed to in<u>ject</u> some life into the party, so I _____ out a joke about the host, and everyone started laughing.

3 Finish the story using the word parts below. Use each word part once. Your knowledge of word parts, as well as the context clues, will help you create the correct words. If you do not understand the meaning of a word you have made, check the dictionary for the definition or to see whether the word exists.

WORD PARTS

lev	ambi	epi	magni	duc
tude	ject	pos	rog	dom

The Space Voyage

Katy was suffering from bore_____, until she met the aliens. She was ab_____ted by the aliens and taken onto their spacecraft. They told her about the _____tude of their mission. They had to repopulate their planet, and they asked her to be a sur_____ate mother for a short time as there were not

enough female beings on their planet. Katy had been feeling a bit de_____ed, and she thought this adventure might cheer her up. The creatures were _____guous about how far they had to travel on the ship. They said time didn't have any re_____ance in their world.

Katy enjoyed her time with the aliens, and they continually showed their grati_____ by bringing her gifts, but she began to miss her family and friends. She wondered whether her family and friends thought she was dead and what _____taph they had put on her tombstone. Finally, to dis_____e of her worries, the aliens put Katy back on the spaceship and sent her home.

4 Pick the best definition for each underlined word using your knowledge of word parts. Circle the word part in each of the underlined words.

a. the quality of being complete

b. love of learning and literary texts

c. one who provides massage as a job

d. disease spread upon many people

e. regarding humans as the center of the universe

f. high-minded; noble

g. a raised area of earth along a river

h. a lone ruler, by oneself

i. claiming superior rights

j. examination of a body after death

_____ 1. The masseur had strong hands.

_____ 2. The levee wasn't high enough to keep the water from flooding the houses.

_____ 3. The postmortem revealed that the man had been poisoned.

_____ 4. The arrogant man demanded everything done his way.

_____ 5. The magnanimous donation helped us build the hospital sooner than we expected.

_____ 6. The epidemic almost wiped out the small village.

_____ 7. Our anthropocentric views have led to the disappearance of too many plants and animals.

_____ 8. The autocrat began to worry when he heard people complaining about his policies.

_____ 9. We have a plentitude of food for dinner with the pizza I got and the chicken you brought.

_____ 10. Someone who is interested in philology had better like libraries!

5 A good way to remember word parts is to pick one word that uses a word part and understand how that word part functions in the word. Then you can apply that meaning to other words that have the same word part. Use the words to help you match the word part to its meaning.

SET ONE

_____ 1. **ambi-, amphi-:** ambiguous, amphibian, ambivalent

_____ 2. **magni-:** magnificent, magnify, magnitude

_____ 3. **-anthro-:** anthropology, philanthropy, anthropocentric

_____ 4. **-ject-:** inject, conjecture, eject

_____ 5. **-eur:** entrepreneur, masseur, connoisseur

a. one who

b. to throw

c. human

d. both, around

e. great, large

SET TWO

_____ 6. **auto-:** autograph, autonomy, automation

_____ 7. **-lev-:** levity, levitate, elevator

_____ 8. **-phil-:** philosophy, philanthropy, bibliophile

_____ 9. **-rog-:** interrogate, derogatory, arrogant

_____ 10. **-tude:** magnitude, gratitude, aptitude

f. lift, light, rise

g. state or quality of

h. love

i. self

j. to ask

HINT

Etymologies

An etymology is the history of a word. Some dictionaries will explain at the end of an entry how the word came into existence. Words can be developed in several ways such as being made up, coming from a person's name, or evolving from foreign languages. Reading a word's etymology can sometimes help you remember the meaning. For example, the word **dismal** comes from the Latin *dies mali. Dies* is the plural of day and *mali* the plural of evil. In Middle English the word meant unlucky days; there were two days in each month that were thought to be unfavorable. The word now means "causing depression or dread." It is easy to see how this definition came from the idea of unlucky days. Not all words have interesting histories, but taking the time to read an etymology can be useful. If you get excited about word origins, there are books available on the subject that show how fascinating language can be.

6 Use the dictionary to find a word you don't know that uses the word part. Write the meaning of the word part, the word, and the definition. If your dictionary has the etymology (history) of the word, see how the word part relates to the meaning, and write the etymology after the definition.

Word Part	Meaning	Word	Definition and Etymology
EXAMPLE:			
magni-	great, large	magnifico	1. a Venetian nobleman
			2. any person of high rank. from Latin
			magnificus, magn(us) large, great
1. ambi-			
2. epi-			
3. post-			
4. anthro-			
5. phil-			

CHAPTER

6 Chemistry

From Ancient to Modern Times

Chemistry is a science that has had an influence on society from the ancient Egyptians to the modern day. Among the first chemical experiments were those done by **alchemists**. From 300 B.C. to about A.D. 1700, al-
5 chemists conducted various experiments. Two of their major goals were to change inexpensive metals such as lead into gold and to find the **elixir** of life, a drink they believed would lead to eternal life. They were not successful with either **endeavor**, but they did begin the
10 foundation of chemical experiments. They created symbols for various substances and developed methods of **distilling** and purifying various chemical compounds. Their experiments helped in discovering the essential qualities of some chemicals.

15 Today, chemistry is used in areas from **forensics** to food. Chemistry has been valuable in the field of forensics in **analyzing** samples of blood and hair from crime scenes. For example, in the 1960s an historian suspected foul
20 play in Napoleon's death in 1821 on the island of St. Helena. His body was **exhumed** and a hair sample taken. Because hair doesn't decay, scientists were able to do chemical studies on it
25 checking for **toxic** substances. **Traces** of arsenic were found in Napoleon's hair, which led to the possible conclusion that he was poisoned at the age of fifty-one.
30 Chemistry has also aided in detecting **carcinogens** in food and food additives. Among the cancer-causing agents that chemists discovered through experiments with lab animals were cyclamates (artificial sweeteners). After several years of testing, the Food and Drug Administration (FDA) banned cyclamates in 1970.
35 Obviously, chemistry has a long history and is present in our everyday lives in many ways.

▋▎▍ PREDICTING

Cover the Word List below as you do the Predicting exercise. For each set, write the definition on the line next to the word to which it belongs. If you are unsure, return to the reading on page 31, and underline any context clues you find. After you've made your predictions, uncover the Word List and check your answers. Place a checkmark in the boxes next to the words whose definitions you missed. These are the words you'll want to study closely.

SET ONE

extracting elements   an attempt   medical knowledge used in law
a chemist of the Middle Ages   a drink thought to prolong life

☐ 1. **alchemist** (line 4) _____

☐ 2. **elixir** (line 7) _____

☐ 3. **endeavor** (line 9) _____

☐ 4. **distilling** (line 12) _____

☐ 5. **forensics** (line 15) _____

SET TWO

cancer-causing agents   poisonous   examining   a small amount   dig up

☐ 6. **analyzing** (line 17) _____

☐ 7. **exhume** (line 22) _____

☐ 8. **toxic** (line 25) _____

☐ 9. **traces** (line 25) _____

☐ 10. **carcinogens** (line 31) _____

▋▎▍ WORD LIST

alchemist
[al′ kə mist]

n. a person who practices alchemy (a type of chemistry popular in the Middle Ages)

analyze
[an′ ə līz′]

v. 1. to examine carefully
2. to separate a material into its basic parts

carcinogen
[kär sin′ ə jən, jen′]

n. any cancer-producing substance

distill
[dis til′]

v. 1. to concentrate or separate by distillation
2. to extract the essential elements
3. to fall in drops; to trickle

elixir
[i lik′ sər]

n. 1. an alchemic preparation believed capable of prolonging life indefinitely
2. a sweetened solution used in medicine

endeavor
[en dev′ ər]

n. an attempt
v. to make an effort; to try

exhume
[ig zoom′, eks hyoom′]

v. 1. to dig up something buried in the earth (especially a dead body)
2. to revive after a period of forgetting

forensics
[fə ren′ siks]

n. 1. a department of forensic medicine (the use of medical knowledge in civil or criminal law), as in a police laboratory
2. the study of formal debate

toxic
[tok ′ sik]

adj. 1. caused by a poison
2. poisonous

trace
[trās]

n. 1. an extremely small amount of a substance
2. evidence of some former action or event
v. to follow the history of; to discover

1 Match the vocabulary word to the words you could associate with it.

_____	1. elixir	a. crimes, techniques
_____	2. distill	b. try, effort
_____	3. forensics	c. deadly, lethal
_____	4. toxic	d. dig up, uncover
_____	5. carcinogen	e. gold, Middle Ages
_____	6. alchemist	f. small, evidence
_____	7. endeavor	g. separate, essential
_____	8. analyze	h. drink, magic
_____	9. exhume	i. cancer, substance
_____	10. trace	j. study, examine

2 Finish the sentences. Use each word once.

VOCABULARY LIST

toxic	forensics	endeavor	elixir	distill
analyzed	trace	alchemist	exhume	carcinogens

1. I drink so many sodas that my friends think I see them as the _____ of life.
2. When we toured the _____ lab, we saw some of the equipment used to test blood and hair samples.
3. I was reading a mystery novel and was surprised by what could be combined with cologne to make a(n) _____ substance.
4. The family wanted to _____ Uncle Les when they thought he had been buried with Grandma Allison's hearing aid in his pocket.
5. The _____ worked late into the night trying different chemicals on the bar of lead, but it was still lead in the morning.
6. Scientists are still unsure of all the substances that are _____, but they range from overcooked meat to gasoline.
7. There wasn't a(n) _____ of evidence that Erik had been at the scene of the crime, but the police held him overnight anyway.
8. After doing the experiment, I _____ my lab report to see whether I could tell why I didn't get the expected result.
9. I will _____ to improve my grades by studying more every night.
10. Before the judge could make her decision, she had to _____ all the information the witnesses had given her.

3 Answer each question by writing the vocabulary word on the line next to the example it best fits. Use each word once.

VOCABULARY LIST

alchemist	carcinogen	elixir	exhume	toxic
analyze	distill	endeavor	forensics	trace

1. If Matthew says he will try to make it to your party, what will he do? _____

2. The police had to dig up the body after they suspected murder as the cause of death. What did they do to the body? _____

3. Gasoline has been labeled a cancer-causing substance. What is it? _____

4. At 75, Milton looked the same as he did at 25. His friends thought he had found the secret to long life. What did they think he had discovered? _____

5. June decided she wanted to learn how to debate. What kind of class did she decide to take?

   _____

6. The gas that escaped from the factory made six of the workers seriously ill, and they were rushed to the hospital. What quality did the gas have? _____

7. In chemistry lab, Keri had to separate one chemical from another. How did she do this?

   _____

8. Simon, a young man who lived in the 1400s, experimented with chemicals to try to find a way to live forever. What was his occupation? _____

9. For her law class, Katy was given a court case and asked to study how the jury made its decision. What did she have to do to the case? _____

10. Karl is going to follow his family's journey from Sweden to America in the late 1800s. What is he going to do with his family's history? _____

Notice how the vocabulary words are used on the form and in the background information below. Use as many of the vocabulary words as you can to complete the report.

Background Information: Mr. Harvey Watson's family has come to suspect murder in his sudden death. They have asked that his body be exhumed and analyzed for toxic substances. The day before Watson's death he spent the morning working in his garden, and in the afternoon he spent several hours in his lab where he practiced alchemy. That night he ate a large dinner and drank heavily. Watson was fifty years old and had no known health problems. The family requests that every endeavor be made to distill the facts as to what could have caused Watson's untimely demise.

Forensics Lab Report

Examiner _____

Date _____

1. Name of the person exhumed: _____

2. Reason for the exhumation: _____

3. Unusual substances found in analyzing the body: _____

_____

4. Amount of substances found: _____

5. Final analysis as to the cause of death: _____

_____

7 Sociology

Greetings, All

Greetings are a **socialization** behavior that most people take for granted because greetings are so **pervasive** in society. But from a young age, people are taught the appropriate greetings for different circumstances. Studying everyday life can help us better understand why we act the ways we do. Sociologist Erving Goffman points out that greetings are part of our face-to-face contacts, phone con-

5 versations, and letters. Two important areas that greetings illuminate are **status** and cultural differences. For example, which person says "hello" first and how someone is greeted can be part of the **stratification** system in a society. In the past, a man removed his hat

10 and bowed to greet a prince or king; this behavior showed his lower rank in the society. This greeting became truncated over time. Later, people began to greet equals by just lifting the hat, and then by touching the hat. Finally, a motion toward the hat was enough of a

15 greeting among friends.

Greeting rules also vary by country. In France, people kiss each other on the cheek as a friendly, everyday greeting, but this type of behavior is not the **norm** in the United States. Mahadev Apte explored

20 another cultural difference in the use of "thank you" forms in the South Asian languages of Hindi and Marathi. In these cultures, a "thank you" form is essential in public ceremonies and in introductions to books, but thank yous are **taboo** with family members,

25 close friends, or in business transactions. In some cultures, people may be **ostracized** for not following proper greeting behavior. In fact, knowing what is forbidden and accepted has become important in international business, as a mistake in greeting rituals can

30 ruin a business deal or a company.

Deviating from **conventional** greeting behavior can lead to problems. For example, linguist C. A. Ferguson, as an informal experiment, didn't respond to his secretary's "good morning" for two days in a row. He reported that the atmosphere was unpleasant on the first day and tense on the second day. By the third day, to **alleviate** the stress and save their working relationship, he discon-

35 tinued the experiment. Obviously, what people say and do in what may seem like simple everyday greetings can have more relevance than people imagine.

■■■ PREDICTING

Cover the Word List below as you do the Predicting exercise. For each set, write the definition on the line next to the word to which it belongs. If you are unsure, return to the reading on page 36, and underline any context clues you find. After you've made your predictions, uncover the Word List and check your answers. Place a checkmark in the boxes next to the words whose definitions you missed. These are the words you'll want to study closely.

SET ONE

social standing   a standard   the act of developing levels of class   a learning process having the quality to spread

- ❏ 1. **socialization** (line 1) _____
- ❏ 2. **pervasive** (line 2) _____
- ❏ 3. **status** (line 6) _____
- ❏ 4. **stratification** (line 8) _____
- ❏ 5. **norm** (line 19) _____

SET TWO

to exclude   to relieve   a prohibition   moving away from   customary

- ❏ 6. **taboo** (line 24) _____
- ❏ 7. **ostracize** (line 26) _____
- ❏ 8. **deviating** (line 31) _____
- ❏ 9. **conventional** (line 31) _____
- ❏ 10. **alleviate** (line 34) _____

■■■ WORD LIST

alleviate
[ə le′ vē āt′]
v. to relieve; to reduce

conventional
[kən ven′ shən əl]
adj. 1. customary
2. conforming to established standards

deviate
[dē′ vē āt′]
v. 1. to move away from a norm or set behavior
2. to cause to turn aside or to differ

norm
[nôrm]
n. a standard or pattern regarded as typical for a specific group

ostracize
[os′ trə sīz′]
v. to exclude, by general consent, from society or from privileges

pervasive
[pər vā′ siv, ziv]
adj. having the quality to spread throughout or permeate

socialization
[so′ shə li zā′ shən]
n. the process whereby an individual learns the values and behaviors appropriate to his or her culture and social standing

status
[stā′ təs, stat′ əs]
n. 1. a relative position; standing, especially social standing
2. high standing
3. situation

stratification
[strat′ ə fi kā′ shən]
n. the act or process of developing levels of class or privilege

taboo
[tə bōō′, ta-]
n. a prohibition excluding something from use or mention
v. to exclude from use

1 Circle the word that best completes each sentence.

1. Instead of using the (conventional, pervasive) entrance, my brother likes to enter the house through his bedroom window.

2. To (deviate, alleviate) the pain, Elizabeth put ice on her sore knee.

3. I kept asking about the (norm, status) of the flight, but no one at the check-in counter was sure when the plane would take off.

4. It is usually considered (taboo, norm) to ask how much money a person makes.

5. When no one got a raise, discontent was the (conventional, pervasive) mood in the office.

6. I enrolled my son in preschool to help his (socialization, stratification).

7. We had to (deviate, alleviate) from the syllabus because it was worthwhile to attend the assembly.

8. In some countries, such as India, (stratification, taboo) has been very important to how people are treated.

9. It is considered the (norm, taboo) to tip waiters in the United States, but that is not the custom in all countries.

10. Sarah was (ostracized, alleviated) from the cooking club when she brought in a peanut butter and jelly sandwich and called it gourmet food.

2 Put a T for true or F for false next to each statement.

_____ 1. A group might consider ostracizing someone with an unpleasant odor.

_____ 2. Ox-drawn carts are pervasive in American society.

_____ 3. A massage can help to alleviate stress.

_____ 4. One's status in society is often determined by one's job.

_____ 5. Spending the weekend skiing in Switzerland is the norm for most students.

_____ 6. Riding a pogo stick is a conventional method of transportation.

_____ 7. Blowing bubbles with one's gum is considered taboo in the classroom.

_____ 8. There is no type of stratification in the military.

_____ 9. A flooded road can cause people to deviate from an intended route.

_____ 10. Socialization can take place at the dinner table.

3 Finish the reading using the vocabulary words. Use each word once.

VOCABULARY LIST

alleviate	norm	pervasive	conventional	socialization
status	taboo	deviate	ostracized	stratification

Fitting In

The years spent in school are certainly an important part of the (1)_____ process. It is during school hours that children learn how to get along with others and how different groups act. Certainly (2)_____ is part of the schoolyard. Some

students are the "in" group and have special privileges, while others are considered "outsiders." One's (3)_____ in school can help determine whether one is invited to parties or teased during recess. Those who (4)_____ from the accepted standards, whether by wearing out-of-style clothes or not keeping up on the latest slang, can expect to be criticized. In extreme cases these students may even be (5)_____. What is considered right and wrong can change quickly. One week it may be (6)_____ to wear stripes, and the next week stripes can be all the rage.

To (7)_____ the stress of trying to fit in, parents should give their children love and encouragement at home. The need to fit in, however, is (8)_____ in society, so parents should balance accepting some requests for the latest gadgets with giving in to every childhood whim. What was the (9)_____ when parents went to school and what is the standard today can vary greatly, and parents must be willing to change their ideas of what is and isn't acceptable. The (10)_____ wisdom that "father knows best" may not always hold true in a rapidly changing world.

INTERACTIVE EXERCISE

Give two examples for each of the following.

1. Where can you see socialization taking place?

   _____   _____

2. What are pervasive problems in today's society?

   _____   _____

3. What jobs have a high status in American society?

   _____   _____

4. What institutions use stratification?

   _____   _____

5. What situations might cause someone to deviate from his or her regular behavior?

   _____   _____

6. What norms are found in the classroom?

   _____   _____

7. What topics are usually considered taboo at dinner parties?

   _____   _____

8. Why might someone be ostracized from a group?

   _____   _____

9. What are conventional Mother's Day gifts?

   _____   _____

10. What do you do to alleviate pain when you are sick?

   _____   _____

8 Composition

Exploring an Issue

Community Research Project

First Draft Due: April 8

Final Draft Due: May 1

5 Your assignment is to pick a problem in the community and research ways to resolve it. For example, you might study the need for more parking downtown, how to deal with freeway traffic, or how to improve the county recycling program. There are numerous areas to explore.

10 • Make your **thesis** clear in the first paragraph of your paper. Readers should understand the point you want to make.

• Add a **refutation** section to your paper. Look at other sides of the issue and show how your plan is better than theirs.

• Your **intention** is to help the community by noting the problem and presenting a valid
15 solution.

In writing the paper, remember the important concepts we have covered this semester.

• **coherence**: all the examples in your paper should relate to your thesis.

• **diction**: your choice of words should reflect your purpose and knowledge of your audience. Remember this is a formal paper. Be aware of the **denotations** (dictionary definitions) and
20 **connotations** (the feelings and emotions words take on) of the words you use. The different meanings will influence your readers.

• **transitions**: transitions help your writing flow. You can use transition words, such as however, then, next, and first (see your writing text for more examples), repeat key words, or use **parallelism**. Remember putting lists in the same structure makes your writing flow.
25 (Examples: My hobbies are reading, writing, and swimming; I like to read, to write, and to swim).

• Include at least three quotations and three **paraphrases** in the proper format as discussed in class. Remember to put the page number where you found the quote in parentheses.

30 Quotation: use the writer's own words and put the words in quotation marks.

Example: E. M. Forster states, "Property makes its owner feel that he ought to do something to it" (64).

Paraphrase: put the writer's words into your own words and do not use quotation marks.

Example: In writing about buying some woodland, E. M. Forster feels that one of the effects
35 the land has on him is making him want to change it in some way (64).

As you write the paper, have fun finding out about the community and helping to solve one of its problems.

Cover the Word List below as you do the Predicting exercise. For each set, write the definition on the line next to the word to which it belongs. If you are unsure, return to the reading on page 41, and underline any context clues you find. After you've made your predictions, uncover the Word List and check your answers. Place a checkmark in the boxes next to the words whose definitions you missed. These are the words you'll want to study closely.

SET ONE

a plan   consistency   the act of disproving a statement
a proposition that is defended by argument   the choice and use of words

❑ 1. **thesis** (line 10) _____

❑ 2. **refutation** (line 12) _____

❑ 3. **intention** (line 14) _____

❑ 4. **coherence** (line 17) _____

❑ 5. **diction** (line 18) _____

SET TWO

the suggestive meaning of a word   the direct meaning of a word   the process of changing
the use of corresponding syntactical forms   a restatement of a passage using other words

❑ 6. **denotation** (line 19) _____

❑ 7. **connotation** (line 20) _____

❑ 8. **transition** (line 22) _____

❑ 9. **parallelism** (line 24) _____

❑ 10. **paraphrase** (line 27) _____

▌▌▌ WORD LIST

coherence
[kō hēr′ əns, kō her′-]
n. consistency; the quality of a logical or orderly relationship of parts

connotation
[kon′ ə tā′ shən]
n. the suggestive or associative meaning of a term beyond its literal definition

denotation
[dē′ nō tā′ shən]
n. the explicit or direct meaning of a word

diction
[dik′ shən]
n. 1. the choice and use of words in speech or writing
2. distinctness of speech

intention
[in ten′ shən]
n. 1. a plan; an aim that guides action

parallelism
[par′ ə lel iz′ əm]
n. 1. the use of corresponding syntactical forms
2. likeness or similarity in aspect

paraphrase
[par′ ə frāz′]
n. a restatement of a passage using other words
v. to express in a paraphrase

refutation
[ref′ yoo tā′ shən]
n. 1. the act of disproving a statement or argument
2. something that refutes

thesis
[thē′ sis]
n. a proposition that is defended by argument

transition
[tran zish′ ən]
n. 1. the process of changing from one form or activity to another
2. passage from one subject to another

▌▌▌ SELF-TESTS

1 Circle the correct meaning of each vocabulary word.

1. connotation:	direct meaning	suggestive meaning
2. diction:	choice of words	choice of type size
3. parallelism:	contrast in parts	similarity in aspects
4. paraphrase:	to use an author's words	to express in other words
5. refutation:	disproving a statement	agreeing with a statement
6. transition:	staying in the same place	process of changing
7. coherence:	illogical organization	orderly relationship
8. denotation:	suggestive meaning	direct meaning
9. intention:	a plan	clueless
10. thesis:	a proposition	a refusal

2 Match a word to each example.

VOCABULARY LIST

connotation	intention	transition	diction	parallelism
coherence	denotation	paraphrase	refutation	thesis

1. later, while, furthermore, finally _____
2. mother: a female parent _____
3. According to Austen it isn't how long it takes, but how good it is that matters. _____
4. I *really want* a new car. I *desire* a new car. I *need* a new car. _____
5. Over the weekend, the children read books, drew pictures, and made cupcakes.
_____
6. mother: the person who made me cookies and tucked me into bed _____
7. Some people in the company believe the change in policy is causing problems, but they need to look ahead and see that after some initial scheduling problems, all employees will have more time to spend on leisure pursuits. For example, when the rotation begins. . . . _____
8. The school needs to offer more math classes so that students can graduate on time.
_____
9. The plan is to get up at 6:00 and be on the road by 6:30. _____
10. Outline: Summer can cause special problems for some people. _____
    I. A greater chance of getting sunburned
    II. Dehydration
    III. Heat exhaustion

3 Finish the sentences using the vocabulary words. Use each word once.

VOCABULARY LIST

refuted	thesis	parallelism	paraphrase	transition
denotation	diction	coherence	intention	connotations

1. The sentence "I didn't buy the car because the paint was scratched, the windshield was broken, and the ribbed upholstery bothered me" was hard to read because it didn't use _____.

2. The _____ of my research paper is that more Neighborhood Watch programs will make our city safer.

3. Because I was writing for children, I paid extra care to my _____. I didn't want to use words they wouldn't understand.

4. I was confused when reading Isabel's paper because it lacked _____. First she told about a trip to a farm and then she described her math test, and her topic was supposed to be about a favorite building.

5. It can be hard to _____ because you want to get the writer's idea correct, but you can't use any of the writer's key words or the same sentence pattern.

6. When I mentioned the word *dog* in class, I found out that the _____ varied from a cute poodle to a mean Doberman depending on people's experiences.

7. The _____ of the orientation meeting was to help students understand the campus, not to confuse them.

8. I thought my idea for the party was the best, but after Tony _____ my points, I saw how expensive and impractical my plan was.

9. The dictionary helped me with the _____ for the word *love,* but I know that in most people's minds the word means more than "an intense affectionate concern for another person."

10. By using the _____ words *for instance* and *to illustrate,* I remember to put examples in my papers, which makes them more interesting to read.

▮▮▮ INTERACTIVE EXERCISE

Write a paragraph on your attitude toward writing. Use six examples of the vocabulary words in your paragraph. Label the words when you have finished the paragraph. For example, if you write, "After I am done writing, I am usually proud of the hard work I put into it," make an arrow to the transition word *After* and write *transition* in the margin.

_____

_____

_____

_____

_____

_____

_____

_____

_____

9 Theater

Behind the Curtain

Our tour is in luck. Let's stop for a few minutes behind the curtain and listen as our two resident playwrights discuss ideas for this summer's new play.

HENRIK: I've been thinking about the play we are writing, and
5   I'd like the **antagonist** to be a woman named June. I find that it often surprises the audience when a woman is the adversary.

LORRAINE: That's fine with me, Henrik, and I was thinking the **protagonist** should be a woman named Colleen.
10   There aren't enough female leads in the theater.

HENRIK: Sure, having two major female roles will be great for costuming. The play is going to be performed in the large **amphitheater**, so we can use the women's strong personalities to design outfits with dramatic colors that
15   can be easily seen from all the seats. In fact, I think Colleen's **hubris** should be about her appearance. Her pride in her looks will be her major flaw and almost cause her downfall.

LORRAINE: Great idea! I know we aren't writing a tragedy, but we do want some **pathos** in the play. The audience should feel sympathy or pity for both
20   leads. In the **prologue** let's start by telling the audience about the longtime feud between these two women.

HENRIK: Good, we will set up the conflict before the play begins. Then June and Colleen should each have a **monologue** at some point in the play. They should each have a long solo speech to tell their feelings and history.

25 LORRAINE: Who should the **ingénue** be? I was thinking Colleen's sister Alicia would be the perfect innocent young woman. We won't, however, make her so sweet that she steals the **limelight** from the other characters.

HENRIK: No, she shouldn't grab any scenes from the stars. We would still have Colleen speak the **epilogue** where she sums up the play and says
30   something to get the audience applauding.

LORRAINE: Yes, that's it. Now all we have to do is develop the conflict, decide on the climax, write the dialogue, and we've got ourselves a play.

▌▐▌ PREDICTING

Cover the Word List below as you do the Predicting exercise. For each set, write the definition on the line next to the word to which it belongs. If you are unsure, return to the reading on page 45, and underline any context clues you find. After you've made your predictions, uncover the Word List and check your answers. Place a checkmark in the boxes next to the words whose definitions you missed. These are the words you'll want to study closely.

SET ONE

an adversary   arrogance   the leading character   a feeling of sympathy
a round structure having seats rising from an open space in the center

❑   1. **antagonist** (line 5) _____

❑   2. **protagonist** (line 9) _____

❑   3. **amphitheater** (line 13) _____

❑   4. **hubris** (line 16) _____

❑   5. **pathos** (line 19) _____

SET TWO

an innocent girl   a long solo speech   the lines introducing a play
a speech after the conclusion of a play   the focus of attention

❑   6. **prologue** (line 20) _____

❑   7. **monologue** (line 23) _____

❑   8. **ingénue** (line 25) _____

❑   9. **limelight** (line 27) _____

❑ 10. **epilogue** (line 29) _____

▌▐▌ WORD LIST

amphitheater
[am′ fə thē′ ə tər]
n. 1. an oval or round structure having tiers of seats rising outward from an open space in the center
2. an arena where contests are held

antagonist
[an tag′ ə nist]
n. one who opposes and competes with someone else; an adversary

epilogue
[ep′ ə lôg′, log]
n. 1. a short poem or speech spoken directly to the audience after the conclusion of a play
2. a short addition at the end of any literary work, often telling what happens to the characters in the future

hubris
[hyōō′ bris]
n. arrogance; overbearing pride

ingénue
[an′ zhe nōō′, nyōō]
n. 1. an innocent girl or young woman
2. an actress playing an ingénue

limelight
[līm′ līt′]
n. a position as the focus of attention

monologue
[mon′ ə lôg, log]
n. a long speech made by one person, often monopolizing conversation

pathos
[pā′ thos′, thôs′]
n. a feeling of sympathy or pity

prologue
[prō′ lôg′, log′]
n. 1. the lines introducing a play
2. an introductory act or event

protagonist
[prō tag′ ə nist]
n. 1. the leading character in a work of literature
2. any leading or principal figure

1 Put a T for true or F for false next to each statement.

_____ 1. An antagonist in a play might try to blackmail the hero.

_____ 2. An ingénue is likely to punch someone in the face.

_____ 3. If you arrive fifteen minutes late to a play, you have probably missed the epilogue.

_____ 4. You might want a seat cushion in an amphitheater.

_____ 5. During a scene with a sick child, most people would feel pathos.

_____ 6. The protagonist is usually in a play for only ten or fifteen minutes.

_____ 7. After an actor wins an Oscar, he is likely to be in the limelight for a while.

_____ 8. The prologue is usually given just before the first intermission.

_____ 9. A person's hubris can cause him or her to forget about other people's feelings.

_____ 10. Listening to a friend's monologue can be frustrating when you have something you want to say.

2 Finish the reading using the vocabulary words. Use each word once.

VOCABULARY LIST

protagonist	hubris	pathos	ingénue	epilogue
limelight	monologue	antagonist	prologue	amphitheater

Farm Living

When the curtain parts, the (1)_____, Diana, is standing in front of a garden with a smile on her sweet, young face. In the (2)_____ she tells the audience that the play is about how the family farm is going to be taken away from them. Then an evil laugh is heard offstage, and the (3)_____, the cruel and rich Mr. Roth, enters. He opposes Diana's father, Rudolph, the (4)_____ in the play.

Whenever Rudolph bounds onto the stage, he steals the (5)_____. He is so forceful that he can't help but be the center of attention. During his (6)_____ the audience is hushed. Diana too has her moments. She arouses the audience's (7)_____ when she falls, sprains her ankle, and hobbles home to find a sign out front. There isn't a dry eye in the (8)_____, when she cries out, "It's been sold!" In the end, however, Mr. Roth's (9)_____ causes his downfall. He believes in cruelty, and he is shocked when the town rallies behind Diana and Rudolph to get the farm back. The (10)_____ adds the surprising but happy information that Mr. Roth changes his ways and marries Diana.

3 Complete the following analogies. See the Analogies Appendix on page 159 for instructions on how to complete analogies.

1. Black Beauty : horse :: Little Miss Muffet : _____
2. kindness : cruelty :: _____ : friend
3. steering wheel : car :: seat : _____
4. windy day : flower pot falls over :: end of a play : _____
5. comedian : _____ :: chef : mixing bowl
6. a flat tire : a problem :: bride at a wedding : _____
7. forbid : prohibit :: _____ : arrogance
8. cat : pet :: Sherlock Holmes : _____
9. play begins : _____ :: unlock a door : walk in
10. a friend is robbed : _____ :: you win the lottery : happiness

---

HINT

Make Your Own Tests

A great way to study is to make your own tests in the same style of the tests that you will have in class. Making the tests puts you in the instructor's frame of mind and makes you think about what is important to study.

- Before the first test (or quiz), ask your instructor what format(s) the test will be in—true/false, multiple choice, matching, essay.
- Create a test in the same format(s) with questions that you think will be asked, neatly handwritten or typed.
- Set the test aside for a day.
- The next day, take the test and correct yourself. How much did you remember?
- Make a test for a friend and exchange with each other. Did you come up with similar questions?
- If you examine the first in-class test, you will have a better idea of what the instructor is looking for, and then your homemade tests will be even more useful.

INTERACTIVE EXERCISE

Pretend that the play in the reading on page 45 has been finished and performed. You are a reviewer for the local newspaper and have just been to opening night. Write a review of the play that includes a recommendation as to whether or not your readers should see the play. Use at least seven of the vocabulary words in your review.

10 Review

Focus on Chapters 1–9

1. _____

2. _____

3. _____

4. _____

5. _____

6. _____

7. _____

8. _____

9. _____

10. _____

11. _____

12. _____

The following activities give you a chance to interact some more with the vocabulary words you've been learning. By looking at art, acting, writing, taking tests, and doing a crossword puzzle, you will see which words you know well and which you still need to work with.

■■■ ART

Match each picture on page 50 to one of the following vocabulary words. Use each word once.

VOCABULARY LIST

connoisseur	stratification	hail	connotation
destitute	cacophony	philanthropy	exhume
taboo	placate	alchemist	prestigious

■■■ DRAMA

Charades: You will be given one of the following words to act out in class. Think about how this word could be demonstrated without speaking. The other people in class will try to guess what word you are showing.

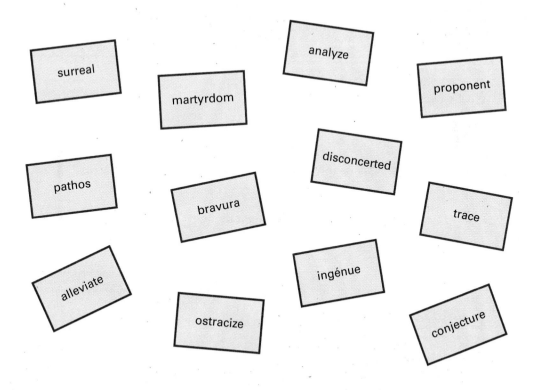

Answer the following questions to further test your understanding of the vocabulary words.

1. What is your favorite genre to read? _____

2. What would be laudable behavior for a child? _____

   _____

3. If an elixir existed that could prolong life forever, would you drink it? Explain why or why not.

   _____

   _____

4. Name two norms for classroom behavior.

   _____

   _____

5. What is one step we can take to stop persecution in society?

   _____

   _____

6. Name a toxic substance._____

7. If decorum was required at a party, describe two ways a person would act.

   _____

   _____

8. Besides looks, in what two other areas might people display their hubris?

   _____

   _____

9. What endeavor have you recently been successful at?

   _____

   _____

10. Name two Olympic sports in which the execution of the activity is scored.

   _____   _____

11. What are two ways people can improve their diction?

   _____

   _____

12. Give the name of the antagonist in a book you have read or a movie you have seen.

   _____

1 Finish the story using the vocabulary words. Use each word once.

VOCABULARY LIST

ambivalence	clamor	feasibility	prestigious
attune	conducive	limelight	status
audible	deviate	magnitude	transition

Not Meant to Be

For once my house was not (1)_____ to studying. Every time I sat down to study, someone started making noise. When my sister turned on the television, I asked her to turn it down, but it was still (2)_____ in my room. After she left, I thought I could get some work done, but my neighbor started a(n) (3)_____. Bob decided it was the perfect time to build the shed he had been talking about for ten years. He was sawing and pounding for hours. My (4)_____ as a top student was quickly falling as the noises around me continued. I saw the (5)_____ Student-of-the-Year Award slip out of my grasp. The (6)_____ of getting all As looked dimmer and dimmer. The (7)_____ of my problems finally hit me: I could fail if I didn't do something right away. I was going to have to (8)_____ from my original plan. With some (9)_____, I turned from my faithful desk where I had spent many happy hours studying and left my room. I was going to have to go to the library and (10)_____ myself to a new environment. The (11)_____ wouldn't be easy, but I was willing to try. I couldn't dream of giving up the (12)_____ I enjoyed in my role as an excellent student. I would adapt to my new circumstances.

2 Pick the word that best completes each sentence.

1. My sister said she needed her _____, so she moved out of our apartment.

   a. feasibility   b. cacophony   c. autonomy   d. cinematography

2. I will do my _____ to make sure you enjoy your vacation while you are staying with me.

   a. taboo   b. utmost   c. endeavor   d. decorum

3. Since its _____ there have been only disagreements on how to operate the policy.

   a. inception   b. bravura   c. montage   d. martyrdom

4. The _____ in the auditorium could be improved: I thought the president of the college said, "Welcome to the graduation cemetery."

   a. genre   b. acoustics   c. alchemist   d. ambivalence

5. Some _____ experiences differ among cultures, such as initiation ceremonies into adulthood.

   a. trace   b. prerogative   c. repertoire   d. socialization

6. I needed to _____ the major points from the textbook and study those areas; I didn't have time to go over everything.

   a. distill   b. attune   c. censure   d. induce

7. The character's _____ was moving; she really explained how sad her childhood had been.

   a. conjecture   b. clamor   c. monologue   d. epitome

8. My grandfather was a real _____. He ran a doughnut shop and a fruit stand.

   a. alchemist   b. proponent   c. carcinogen   d. entrepreneur

9. The _____ of the painting of the starving man next to the one of the king in his finery helped show why the French were upset with the aristocracy.

   a. conjecture   b. cacophony   c. trace   d. juxtaposition

10. The speaker had to _____ his voice as the air conditioning went on and off.

    a. hail   b. modulate   c. induce   d. alleviate

11. The _____ of the play told too much; there was no suspense when the murderer was revealed.

    a. refutation   b. elixir   c. prologue   d. philanthropy

12. The _____ of *work* certainly doesn't cover all the gossiping and fighting I see in my office every day.

    a. ingénue   b. taboo   c. magnitude   d. denotation

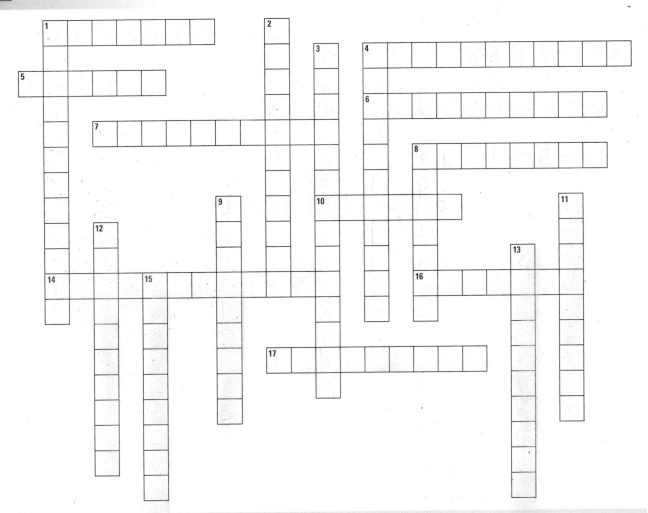

Use the following words to complete the crossword puzzle. You will use each word once.

VOCABULARY LIST

amphitheater	cinematography	epitome	montage	protagonist
ascertain	coherence	forensics	parallelism	refutation
carcinogen	conventional	induce	paraphrase	repertoire
censure	epilogue	intention	prerogative	thesis

Across
1. an official reprimand
4. a special right
5. to persuade
6. the act of disproving a statement
7. a restatement of a passage using other words
8. an addition at the end of a literary work
10. a proposition defended by argument
14. an arena
16. a film editing technique
17. consistency

Down
1. customary
2. principal figure, ex. Indiana Jones or Mary Poppins
3. the art of motion-picture photography
4. likeness or similarity in aspect
8. typical of a whole group
9. a police laboratory
11. to learn with certainty
12. works that an artist can present
13. a cancer-causing substance
15. an aim that guides action

Planning for the Future

$FINANCIAL INSIGHTS

FALL 2004

INVESTMENT REALITIES

When buying stocks or **mutual** funds, keeping a few points in mind will help you be a better investor.

Don't expect to triple your investment in a few months. **Affluence** doesn't just happen; it takes careful planning. For most people, letting one's investments grow over time is the way to get rich.

Remain **resolute** even when the market falters. A **volatile** market can scare people, but changes in the market, even explosive ones, are usual—remain firm. Don't buy and sell without a plan.

Look carefully at the fees **levied** by a broker. Do you pay when you buy or when you sell? Are there monthly or yearly fees? What kinds of transaction fees are imposed?

No one person has a **monopoly** on sound investing. Read the newspaper and business journals to keep up on your investments. Check out books on the stock market or attend a seminar to learn more about how your money can work for you.

MAKE TIME TO MEET

It is a wise person who sets aside time for a **biannual** meeting with a financial advisor to discuss one's **portfolio**. Every six months call your financial planner and ask him or her to meet with you to discuss your holdings.

The following are some questions you will want to consider:

How are my stocks and mutual funds doing? Should I diversify further? What kinds of **fluctuations** have there been in the stock market? If there have been changes in the market, how should I change my investing patterns? How much **equity** do I have in my house? What should I do with that money? How close am I to retirement, and how does that change my investing strategy?

PREDICTING

Cover the Word List below as you do the Predicting exercise. For each set, write the definition on the line next to the word to which it belongs. If you are unsure, return to the reading on page 56, and underline any context clues you find. After you've made your predictions, uncover the Word List and check your answers. Place a checkmark in the boxes next to the words whose definitions you missed. These are the words you'll want to study closely.

SET ONE

wealth   unstable   to impose or to collect   showing firmness   held in common

☐ 1. **mutual** (line 3) _____

☐ 2. **affluence** (line 7) _____

☐ 3. **resolute** (line 12) _____

☐ 4. **volatile** (line 13) _____

☐ 5. **levy** (line 18) _____

biennial — pay B 2 polcu
biannual — 2 p B pilc.

SET TWO

happening twice each year   an irregular variation   exclusive control
the value of a property   a list of investments

☐ 6. **monopoly** (line 23) _____

☐ 7. **biannual** (line 32) _____

☐ 8. **portfolio** (line 33) _____

☐ 9. **fluctuation** (line 41) _____

☐ 10. **equity** (line 45) _____

WORD LIST

affluence
[af′ lo͞o əns]
n. 1. wealth; an abundance
2. a flowing toward

biannual
[bī an′ yo͞o əl]
adj. happening twice each year; semiannual

equity
[ek′ wə tē]
n. 1. the value of a business or property (a house) beyond any mortgage or liability
2. the quality of being fair

fluctuation
[fluk′ cho͞o a′ shən]
n. an irregular variation; the result of such a variation

levy
[lev′ ē]
v. to impose or to collect, such as a tax

monopoly
[mə nop′ ə lē]
n. 1. exclusive control over anything
2. exclusive control by one group of the means of producing or selling a product or service

mutual
[myo͞o′ cho͞o əl]
adj. 1. held in common
2. having the same relationship with each other
3. received in equal amount

portfolio
[pôrt fō′ lē ō′]
n. 1. a list of the investments owned by a bank, investment organization, or other investor
2. a portable case for holding loose sheets of paper or drawings

resolute
[rez′ ə lo͞ot′]
adj. showing firmness; unwavering

volatile
[vol′ ə til]
adj. 1. unstable; changeable
2. threatening to break out into violence; explosive
3. evaporating rapidly

1 In each group, circle the word that does not have a connection to the other three words. See Chapter 3 for an example.

1. mutual	common	diverse	like
2. exclusive	one	shared	monopoly
3. firmness	unchanging	weakness	resolute
4. poor	rich	affluence	abundance
5. semiannual	weekly	twice	biannual
6. impose	levy	collect	give
7. volatile	fleeting	constant	changeable
8. justness	equity	fairness	unequal
9. variation	sameness	fluctuation	change
10. debts	portfolio	holdings	investments

2 Finish the headlines from fictitious newspapers. Use each word once.

VOCABULARY LIST

mutual	resolute	portfolio	volatile	fluctuation
biannual	equity	monopoly	levy	affluence

1. **Despite Pouring Rain, Protestors Remain _____ : They Won't Go Home**

2. **Grocery Wants to _____ Fee for Use of Shopping Carts**

3. *Study Reports _____ of Most Americans Twice as High as Fifty Years Ago*

4. **_____ Discovered in Germany Could Contain Drawings by DaVinci**

5. **County _____ Sale of Overstocked Supplies Offers Deals for Citizens**

6. Wild _____ of Winter Temperatures Spells Disaster for Farmers

7. Part-time Workers Nationwide Look for _____ in Health Benefits

8. Hi-Tech Corporation Charged with Unfair _____ of New Software

9. Parents from Several School Districts Gather to Discuss _____ Problems

10. _____ Political Situation in North Africa Keeps Area Unsafe for Tourists

3 Finish the conversations. Use each word once.

VOCABULARY LIST

fluctuations	resolute	portfolio	volatile	biannual

SET ONE

Changing Needs

"Thank you for calling about our (1) _biannual_ meeting. I am always pleased to go over a client's (2) _portfolio_."

"I have tried to be (3) _resolute_ and not sell my stocks when I see that there has been a plunge in the market, but I am worried."

"It's true that there have been some (4) _fluctuations_ in the market that make it a good idea to change some of your investments. Although it looks like the (5) _volatile_ period is over for a while, we can go over some options to meet your needs."

VOCABULARY LIST

mutual	equity	monopoly	levy	affluence

SET TWO

A Good Investment Choice?

"I'm going to let you in on a great deal. A company has just invented a machine that can suck up all the dust in a house in two minutes. They will have a(n) (6) _monopoly_ on building the machine

for several years. If you invest ten thousand dollars with them now, you will be assured
(7) _affluence_ for life."

"I don't have that much cash handy. Do you think I should use the (8) _equity_ in my house to get a loan?"

"Yes! This deal is not to be missed. I wouldn't recommend this investment to just anyone, but since we have a(n) (9) _mutual_ interest in gardening, I thought I'd help you out. I do have to (10) _levy_ a small fee, just four hundred dollars, for providing you with this tip, but you'll make that back and so much more when the Sucker goes on the market."

HINT

Easy Questions First

If you get stuck on one question, go to the next one. When you finish answering the ones that are easy for you, see which questions and words are left. With fewer choices, the answers should be easier to find.

▌▌▌ INTERACTIVE EXERCISE

Write short responses for each of the following items.

1. Give an example of a mutual interest you and a friend share. _____

2. Tell about a time when you were resolute. _____
_____

3. Name three people who symbolize affluence.
_____   _____   _____

4. Describe a fluctuation you have experienced. _____

5. List two kinds of equity for which workers fight. _____   _____

6. List three situations that could easily become volatile.
_____   _____   _____

7. List two places where a fee might be levied. _____   _____

8. Name two professions where someone would likely carry a portfolio.
_____   _____

9. State two activities that people should do at least biannually.
_____   _____

10. Name two items the government has a monopoly on.
_____   _____

valoies ⟨vɑ'bi:s⟩
ckəg.

The Temples of Angkor

In the jungles of Cambodia sit a **multitude** of temples built during the Khmer Empire between the ninth and thirteenth centuries. Each **successive** king built his own **enclave** consisting of religious temples,
5 administrative buildings, and royal palaces. Each king felt that to **procure** his place in history, he had to build his own temple complex, and about fifty sites have been discovered in the Angkor region. (Angkor means "city" or "capital.") Only religious buildings
10 could be made of stone, and they are the only structures that have survived.

The kings were highly **venerated** and may have been worshiped as gods. Many of the temple statues bear the likeness of the ruling king. The **depictions** of the rulers are also often linked to the current religion, either Hinduism or Buddhism. For example, Jayavarman VII, whose rule began in 1181, had
15 several statues made of himself as a Buddhist god. The statues and temples at Angkor are **potent** symbols of the power of the kings. The temples are huge and beautifully decorated with carvings of religious significance, of a king's achievements, and of scenes of everyday life. At various times over ten thousand people lived at Angkor, including, according to an inscription on one temple complex, "615 dancing girls."

20 The empire began to **wane** in the fourteenth century, and an invasion from Thailand in 1431 led to the destruction of Angkor. The Khmer left the area, never to return. The **profuse** jungle growth reclaimed much of the area and hid it for four hundred years, waiting for **posterity** to discover it again.

Cover the Word List below as you do the Predicting exercise. For each set, write the definition on the line next to the word to which it belongs. If you are unsure, return to the reading on page 61, and underline any context clues you find. After you've made your predictions, uncover the Word List and check your answers. Place a checkmark in the boxes next to the words whose definitions you missed. These are the words you'll want to study closely.

SET ONE

a bounded area   to regard with respect   the quality of being numerous   consecutive
to obtain

❏ 1. **multitude** (line 1) _____

❏ 2. **successive** (line 3) _____

❏ 3. **enclave** (line 4) _____

❏ 4. **procure** (line 6) _____

❏ 5. **venerate** (line 12) _____

SET TWO

powerful   plentiful   to decrease   future generation
a representation in a picture or sculpture

❏ 6. **depiction** (line 13) _____

❏ 7. **potent** (line 15) _____

❏ 8. **wane** (line 20) _____

❏ 9. **profuse** (line 21) _____

❏ 10. **posterity** (line 22) _____

▌▌█ ▌ WORD LIST

depiction
[di pik′ shən]

n. 1. a representation in a picture or sculpture
2. a representation in words; a description

enclave
[en′ klāv, än′]

n. 1. any distinctly bounded area enclosed within a larger area
2. a country or part of a country lying wholly within the boundaries of another

multitude
[mul′ tə tōōd′]

n. 1. the quality of being numerous
2. a great, indefinite number
3. the masses

posterity
[po ster′ ə tē]

n. 1. future generations
2. all of a person's descendants

potent
[pōt′ nt]

adj. 1. powerful
2. having great control or authority

procure
[prō kyoor′, prə]

v. 1. to obtain
2. to bring about

profuse
[prə fyōōs′, prō]

adj. 1. plentiful; overflowing
2. extravagant

successive
[sək ses′ iv]

adj. following in order; consecutive

venerate
[ven′ ə rāt′]

v. to regard with respect and reverence

wane
[wān]

v. 1. to decrease gradually; to decline
2. to approach an end
n. a gradual declining

▰▮▮▰ SELF-TESTS

1 Match each word with its synonym in Set One and its antonym in Set Two.

SYNONYMS

SET ONE

_____ 1. depiction   a. consecutive

_____ 2. profuse   b. future

_____ 3. enclave   c. enclosure

_____ 4. successive   d. abundant

_____ 5. posterity   e. portrayal

ANTONYMS

SET TWO

_____ 6. procure   f. increase

_____ 7. multitude   g. give

_____ 8. venerate   h. degrade

_____ 9. potent   i. few

_____ 10. wane   j. useless

2 Pick the best word to complete each sentence. Use each word once.

VOCABULARY LIST

profuse	waned	multitude	successive	enclave
potent	depicted	procure	venerate	posterity

1. My enthusiasm for the project _waned_ as people began to argue with each other at every meeting.

2. My brother was able to _procure_ two seats to the sold-out concert for us through his business connections.

3. I had to hand my paper in late because of a(n) _multitude_ of problems, from being sick to computer failures.

4. My doctor gave me some _potent_ medicine; I was better in one day.

5. We should _venerate_ our nation's teachers because they have much of the responsibility for educating the future.

6. Her thank-yous were _profuse_, but I didn't feel I deserved that much gratitude.

7. We are vacationing at the Alexander family _enclave_ in the Rocky Mountains. My great-grandfather constructed the cabins and other buildings in the 1800s.

8. I didn't like the way my friend _depicted_ me in his short story. Why was I the villain?

9. Each _successive_ generation has to deal with some of the problems created by the generations who came before.

10. It would be nice if _posterity_ would remember us as a peace-loving people, but the number of wars in the twentieth century probably makes that hope unrealistic.

3 Answer each question with the appropriate vocabulary word. Use each word once.

VOCABULARY LIST

profuse	waned	venerate	successive	enclave
potent	depiction	procure	posterity	multitude

1. Matt has to feed 300 people. What term would describe this group? _multitude_

2. Alexander needs to get food and drinks for the party. What does he need to do?
   procure

3. Colleen thinks her Grandpa is the smartest man in the world. How does she feel about him?
   venerate

4. You can smell a woman's perfume four aisles from you in the movie theater. What word would you use to describe it? _profuse_

5. Most people today want to keep the air and oceans clean. Who are they saving them for?
   posterity

6. We can no longer see our neighbor's front door because the ivy has grown over it. How would you describe the growth in the neighbor's yard? _potent_

7. You see a sculpture of Benjamin Franklin signing *The Declaration of Independence*. What would you call the sculpture? _depiction_

8. After two years of studying biology, it no longer excites Marin. What has happened to her interest in the subject? _waned_

9. Within an hour, Anders stubbed his toe getting out of bed, spilled coffee on himself, and got a flat tire on the way to school. What would you call the problems that happened to him?
   successive

10. At the zoo there is an enclosed area for the primates with an island, a jungle area, and a hospital for newborns. What would this area be called? _enclave_

▌▌▌ INTERACTIVE EXERCISE

Finish the following who, what, where, when, and why lists to practice using the vocabulary words. Give two examples for each question.

1. Where would you find a multitude of people?

   _____   _____

2. Where would you find an enclave of buildings?

   _____   _____

3. What would you procure for a picnic? *obtain*

_____   _____

4. What are some potent smells?

_____   _____

5. Whom do you venerate?

_____   _____

6. Who do you think should be depicted on a coin?

_____   _____

7. Why might a student's attention in class begin to wane?

_____   _____

8. Why should we care about posterity?

_____   _____

9. When would you want to make a profuse apology?

_____   _____

10. When do you need to do something in successive steps?

_____   _____

13 Geography

Adventure Journals

Aug. 5, 1908

As we crossed the desert, I wasn't sure this **escapade** was a good idea. Me, an explorer taking on an adventure into the Australian **hinterlands**? The back country, or Outback, is not a friendly place for humans. The **topography** is unchanging for miles: nothing but flat, dry land. But today we reached Ayers Rock, or Uluru as the Aborigines call it. 5

The red sandstone **monolith** rises 1,143 feet above the plain. And tonight, when I saw the magnificent sight of the monolith changing from red to orange to violet before my eyes, I knew the trip was worth it. The Aborigines have used the rock as a sacred site for centuries. I too have found it an **oasis** in the desert; it is a place filled with mystical power. For days the arid landscape did nothing to endear itself to me, but the sight of the monolith transforming in the sunset has made me love this land. 10

15

July 10, 1953

The **terrain** gets harder every day. The lack of oxygen is beginning to take its toll on me. I'm not sure how much higher I can go. We are
20 nearing 26,000 feet. I've been a **nomad** for years. I've traveled the world trying new experiences and have never been defeated. But I've also never taken on the highest mountain in the world. I'm even beginning to
25 wonder whether I might be suffering from **acrophobia**. No one would believe that I could be afraid of heights, but when I looked down a **ravine** today, I shuddered. I have always considered a bit of fear to be a part of mountain climbing, but my fear is beginning to take over my senses. Could Everest be too much for me? I try to take strength from the confidence of my Sherpa guide, but I'm not sure I can continue. I must dig deep within myself
30 to find the **fortitude** to make it to the top. I must finish!

Cover the Word List below as you do the Predicting exercise. For each set, write the definition on the line next to the word to which it belongs. If you are unsure, return to the reading on page 66, and underline any context clues you find. After you've made your predictions, uncover the Word List and check your answers. Place a checkmark in the boxes next to the words whose definitions you missed. These are the words you'll want to study closely.

SET ONE

the back country   a refuge   the relief features of an area   a reckless adventure
a large single block of stone

❑   1. **escapade** (line 3) _____

❑   2. **hinterlands** (line 5) _____

❑   3. **topography** (line 7) _____

❑   4. **monolith** (line 10) _____

❑   5. **oasis** (line 13) _____

SET TWO

a narrow valley   a wanderer   a fear of heights   mental and emotional strength
a tract of land

❑   6. **terrain** (line 17) _____

❑   7. **nomad** (line 20) _____

❑   8. **acrophobia** (line 25) _____

❑   9. **ravine** (line 26) _____

❑   10. **fortitude** (line 30) _____

▌▌▌ WORD LIST

acrophobia
[ak′ rə fō′ bē ə]
n. a fear of heights

escapade
[es′ kə pād′,
es′ kə pād′]
n. a reckless adventure, especially one contrary to usual or proper behavior

fortitude
[fôr′ ti tōōd′]
n. mental and emotional strength in courageously facing challenges, danger, or temptation

hinterland
[hin′ ter land ′]
n. back country; the remote or less developed parts of a country

monolith
[mon′ ə lith]
n. 1. a large single block of stone
2. a column or large statue formed from a single block of stone
3. something having a uniform, massive, or inflexible character

nomad
[nō′ mad]
n. 1. a wanderer
2. a member of a people who have no permanent home but move from place to place in search of grazing land and food

oasis
[ō ā ′ sis]
n. 1. a refuge, as from work or stress
2. a fertile area in a desert region, usually having a spring or well

ravine
[rə vēn′]
n. a narrow, steep-sided valley, usually eroded by running water

terrain
[tə rān′]
n. a tract of land, especially in reference to its natural features or military advantages

topography
[tə pog′ rə fē]
n. 1. the relief features or surface configuration of an area
2. the detailed description, especially by surveying, of an area

1 Put a T for true or F for false next to each statement.

_____ 1. Someone who has lived in the same house for 40 years would be considered a nomad.

_____ 2. It is dangerous for children to play near ravines.

_____ 3. A person needs fortitude to run a marathon.

_____ 4. If a woman has climbed the 20 highest peaks in North America, she probably has acrophobia.

_____ 5. A teenager's bedroom can be an oasis from the stresses of school and relationships.

_____ 6. A terrain filled with boulders would be easy to ride a bike on.

_____ 7. New York City is considered the hinterlands of the United States.

_____ 8. Deciding to drive across the United States with only $80 in your pocket and no credit cards or other source of money could be considered an escapade.

_____ 9. The topography of Antarctica consists of lush forests and desert areas.

_____ 10. A statue sitting on the corner of a person's desk could be called a monolith.

2 Match each example to the vocabulary word it best fits. Use each word once.

VOCABULARY LIST

| topography | fortitude | nomad | ravine | acrophobia |
| escapade | monolith | oasis | terrain | hinterlands |

1. a statue on Easter Island   _monolith_
2. preparing oneself to speak in front of a crowd   _fortitude_
3. afraid to look over the side of the Empire State Building   _acrophobia_
4. a stand of palm trees in the desert   _oasis_
5. Marco Polo   _nomad_
6. the Yukon in Canada
7. going to the doughnut shop during a blizzard   _escapade_
8. filled with boulders   _terrain_
9. The survey shows that the area contains two hills and a large lake.   _topography_
10. have to leap across one   _ravine_

3 Finish the journal entries using the vocabulary words. Use each word once.

VOCABULARY LIST

nomad	acrophobia	terrain	fortitude	monolith

August 10, 1908

We are preparing to leave the area. I am going to miss it here. Though the

(1) te_____ is flat and inhospitable in so many ways, there is still a mystery and

beauty brought on by the (2) m_____. I climbed to the top of Uluru and was

suprised that I was not afraid. I usually suffer from (3)_____. There is definitely

something special about the place to give me such strength. My (4)_____ has

been tested by the whole journey, and I am proud to say that I have had the power to

withstand the hardships. I do not think I will become a(n) (5)_____ , wandering

the Earth in search of adventure, but I have proved to myself that I can survive and

appreciate the wilds of nature.

SET TWO

VOCABULARY LIST

oasis	escapade	ravine	hinterlands	topography

July 12, 1953

I made it! The last few days have tested my very being. Yesterday we crossed

a(n) (6) r_____ . I slipped and almost fell into it. I thought I was going to die;

I cursed myself for attempting this (7)_____ . But I got my footing and pulled

myself up. When I reached the top of Everest, all the fear and pain were worth it. Now

back in the (8) o_____ of my tent, I have time to relax and reflect. I will not give

up on adventure! But I need a change. This mountainous (9) t_____ has become

too much for me, and I certainly want my next trip to be to some place warmer. The

(10) h_____ of Africa sound appealing right now. What awaits me in the remote

areas of the African jungles? I am anxious to see.

Study Groups

A class can be more rewarding if you find classmates to study with. To create effective study groups, keep these points in mind.

- Get people who really want to learn, not just socialize.
- Pick a time that can accommodate most people; it may be impossible to get every-one together all the time. Exchange e-mail addresses and phone numbers so you can get hold of each other to announce meeting times.
- Decide how often you will meet—twice a week, once a week, once a month.
- Pick a place to meet that is conducive to studying. See whether the library has study group rooms. You want a place where you can talk freely and where you won't be in-terrupted by the telephone, children, or other distractions.
- Bring the necessary books, notes, and other materials to each session.
- Ask various group members to be "the expert" on different chapters or areas of study—have them share their in-depth study with the other group members. Give everyone a chance to participate and respect each person's views. As the semester progresses find each person's strength.
- Assign someone to keep the group on track and be aware of time limits. Gently remind people who start to talk about other topics that you are all there to study.
- Evaluate how useful the session was and decide what changes may be needed for the next time. Try to make the study sessions fun and productive.

▌▐▐▌ INTERACTIVE EXERCISE

Describe possible qualities for each vocabulary word by listing two more adjectives.

1. acrophobia: mild _____ _____

2. ravine: deep _____ _____

3. oasis: lush _____ _____

4. hinterlands: wild _____ _____

5. monolith: huge _____ _____

6. topography: undulating _____ _____

7. fortitude: weakening

_____

_____

8. terrain: rocky

_____

_____

9. nomad: lonely

_____

_____

10. escapade: dangerous

_____

_____

14 Speech

Tips for Any Occasion

Speeches come in various forms. You may need to inform, persuade, or entertain your audience. You may have had weeks or months to prepare, or you may have to give an **impromptu** speech with little or no time to gather your thoughts. You could
5 give a speech to ten good friends or before thousands of strangers. You might be asked to speak at a wedding or a board meeting. The following are some tips you can use for any kind of speaking engagement.

If it is appropriate to your topic and audience, using **levity**
10 to begin a speech can help you and your audience to relax. By telling a joke or an amusing **anecdote**, you may find that you win your audience over in the first few minutes. People enjoy hearing stories, and when the stories are about the speaker, they can be particularly effective.

15 As you plan your speech, make sure your examples are **relevant** to your topic. You should use examples that deal with the subject you are talking about. For example, if your speech

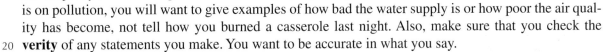

is on pollution, you will want to give examples of how bad the water supply is or how poor the air quality has become, not tell how you burned a casserole last night. Also, make sure that you check the
20 **verity** of any statements you make. You want to be accurate in what you say.

Another way to support your statements is by using expert **testimony**. Find people who are authorities on your topic, and quote them to back up your views. Before you use those people as sources, find out what their credentials are and whether other people in the profession respect them.

Think about the **ramifications** of your statements. What impact will your comments have on your
25 listeners? Also beware of making **derogatory** statements. You shouldn't belittle your listeners or make negative statements about gender, race, or other characteristics.

A technique that can make your speech vivid is **visualization**. Use words that will help listeners see what you are talking about. Describe the people and places that are important to your speech by using sensory details. Tell how something sounded, smelled, or tasted.

30 Lastly, don't forget a **summation** that covers your main points. Remember that your closing is your last chance to reach your audience. If there is something you want them to remember, tell them once again. Give your speech a sense of conclusion. Don't leave your audience feeling that something is missing.

Using these simple techniques can help you feel more confident any time you are asked to step up
35 to the podium.

Cover the Word List below as you do the Predicting exercise. For each set, write the definition on the line next to the word to which it belongs. If you are unsure, return to the reading on page 71, and underline any context clues you find. After you've made your predictions, uncover the Word List and check your answers. Place a checkmark in the boxes next to the words whose definitions you missed. These are the words you'll want to study closely.

SET ONE

to-the-point   a short account   spontaneous   the quality of being real or correct
lightness

❑   1. **impromptu** (line 3) _____

❑   2. **levity** (line 9) _____

❑   3. **anecdote** (line 11) _____

❑   4. **relevant** (line 16) _____

❑   5. **verity** (line 20) _____

SET TWO

proof   insulting   a concluding statement   a development
the formation of a mental image

❑   6. **testimony** (line 21) _____

❑   7. **ramification** (line 24) _____

❑   8. **derogatory** (line 25) _____

❑   9. **visualization** (line 27) _____

❑ 10. **summation** (line 30) _____

■■■ WORD LIST

anecdote
[an' ik dōt']
n. 1. a short account of an interesting or humorous incident
2. secret particulars of history or biography

derogatory
[di rog' ə tôr' ē]
adj. detracting or disparaging; critical; insulting

impromptu
[im promp' tŏŏ]
adj. not rehearsed; spontaneous

levity
[lev' ə tē]
n. 1. lightness of speech or manner; frivolity
2. lightness; buoyancy
3. changeableness

ramification
[ram' ə fə kā' shən]
adj. 1. a development growing out of and often complicating a problem, plan, or statement
2. the act of branching out

relevant
[rel' ə vənt]
adj. pertinent; to-the-point

summation
[sə ma' shən]
n. 1. a concluding statement containing a summary of principal points
2. the act of totaling; addition

testimony
[tes' tə mō' nē]
n. evidence in support of a fact or assertion; proof

verity
[ver' ə tē]
n. 1. the quality of being real, accurate, or correct
2. a statement of principle considered to be permanent truth

visualization
[vizh' ŏŏ ə li za ' shən]
n. the formation of a mental image or images

1 Match each word with its synonym in Set One and its antonym in Set Two.

SYNONYMS

SET ONE

_____ 1. summation   a. image

_____ 2. testimony   b. result

_____ 3. visualization   c. addition

_____ 4. ramification   d. story

_____ 5. anecdote   e. proof

ANTONYMS

SET TWO

_____ 6. verity   f. supportive

_____ 7. levity   g. unrelated

_____ 8. relevant   h. seriousness

_____ 9. derogatory   i. planned

_____ 10. impromptu   j. untrue

2 Circle the word that correctly completes each sentence.

1. When I want to relax, I use (testimony, visualization) to picture myself sleeping in a meadow filled with flowers.

2. My sister told me a funny (ramification, anecdote) about trying to get her son to bed.

3. I have to give a(n) (impromptu, derogatory) speech tomorrow; I hope my instructor gives me a subject I know at least a little about.

4. We needed some (levity, testimony) in the room after Steve spent half an hour telling us about his gallbladder operation.

5. I got up and left the meeting when the speaker started to make (relevant, derogatory) statements about my college.

6. I wanted to believe the man's (anecdote, testimony), but the way he kept mumbling made me think he was lying.

7. In her (levity, summation), the mayor reviewed the major plans for the next year of her term.

8. I wasn't sure about the (ramification, verity) of the speaker's assertion that the moon is one hundred miles from the Earth.

9. I need to find a book on snakes because I think it will have (relevant, impromptu) examples for my talk on dangerous animals.

10. The (ramification, visualization) of arriving twenty minutes late didn't hit me until I looked at the timetable and saw that we would miss the ferry.

3 Use the vocabulary words to complete the following analogies. For instructions on how to complete analogies, see the Analogies Appendix on page 159.

VOCABULARY LIST

levity	testimony	anecdote	visualization	summation
derogatory	verity	impromptu	relevant	ramification

1. consumer : customer :: story : _____
2. complimentary : you have a beautiful home :: _____ : what an ugly house
3. bought a new sweater : purchase :: the sun is hot : _____
4. insult : anger :: joke : _____
5. escape : disappearance :: branching out : _____
6. exercise : take a long walk :: _____ : picture a sunny beach
7. unconnected : unrelated :: pertinent : _____
8. charity : I gave fifty dollars to the Cancer Society :: _____ : I saw him rob the bank
9. intended : planned :: _____ : spontaneous
10. first : last :: opening : _____

▌▐▌▌ INTERACTIVE EXERCISE

Pretend that you are preparing a speech on why the cafeteria needs better food. Make your answers to all but Question 10 deal with this topic.

1. Write an anecdote you could begin your speech with.

   _____
   _____

2. Give two examples that would be relevant to this topic.

   _____   _____

3. Who could give expert testimony on food? _____

4. Explain one way you could check on the verity of the manager's statement: "Providing healthy food is just too expensive for the cafeteria."

   _____

5. In using visualization, to which two senses would you want to appeal the most?

   _____   _____

6. How could you add levity to your talk?

   _____
   _____

7. What might be one ramification of your speech?

    _____

    _____

8. What type of derogatory statement should you avoid using?

    _____

    _____

9. Write a sentence that would be part of your summation.

    _____

    _____

10. If you had to give an impromptu talk about something, on what topic would you speak?

    _____

    _____

15 Word Parts II

Look for words with these **prefixes**, **roots**, and/or **suffixes** as you work through this book. You may have already seen some of them, and you will see others in later chapters. Learning basic word parts can help you figure out the meanings of unfamiliar words.

prefix: a word part added to the beginning of a word that changes the meaning of the root

root: a word's basic part with its essential meaning

suffix: a word part added to the end of a word; indicates the part of speech

WORD PART	MEANING	EXAMPLES AND DEFINITIONS
Prefixes		
bi-	two	*biannual:* happening twice each year *bicycle:* a vehicle with two wheels
mono-	one	*monopoly:* control by one group *monolith:* one block of stone
multi-	many, much	*multitude:* an indefinite number; many *multicolored:* many-colored
prot-	first, primary	*protagonist:* the leading or primary figure *protein:* molecules making up a primary part of every life-form
tri-	three	*triumvirate:* rule by three people *triangle:* a figure with three sides
Roots		
-flu-, -flux-	to flow	*influx:* an act of flowing in *superfluous:* overflowing; excessive
-fus-	to pour	*profuse:* plentiful; pouring in *infuse:* to introduce, as if by pouring
-her-, -hes-	to stick	*coherent:* sticking to one point *adherent:* a person who sticks to a belief
-plac-	to please	*placate:* to please; to calm *placid:* pleasantly calm
-port-	to carry	*portfolio:* a case for carrying papers or drawings *portable:* easy to carry
-sta-, -sti-	to stand, to be in a place	*status:* standing; social position *destitute:* lacking; without support or standing

WORD PART	MEANING	EXAMPLES AND DEFINITIONS
-ver-	truth	*verity:* the quality of being true *veracity:* telling the truth
Suffixes		
-ade (makes a noun)	action or process	*escapade:* the action of a reckless adventure *promenade:* the process of taking a walk
-most (makes an adjective)	most	*utmost:* the most extreme *foremost:* the most important
-phobia (makes a noun)	fear of	*acrophobia:* a fear of heights *claustrophobia:* a fear of enclosed places

▌▌▌▌ SELF-TESTS

1 Read each definition and choose the appropriate word. Use each word once. The meaning of the word part is underlined to help you make the connection. Refer to the Word Parts list if you need help.

VOCABULARY LIST

trilogy	fluid	blockade	complacent	bifocal
monotone	export	verify	anthrophobia	stationary

1. of an eyeglass, having <u>two</u> portions   bifocal
2. <u>pleased</u> with oneself often without an awareness of some problem   complacent *самодовольный*
3. a substance that is capable of flowing   fluid
4. to prove the <u>truth</u> of   verity
5. a vocal utterance in <u>one</u> unvaried sound   monotone
6. the <u>action</u> of obstructing passage or progress   blockade
7. a <u>fear of</u> people   anthrophobia
8. to <u>carry</u> out of a country   export
9. a series of <u>three</u> plays, novels, movies, etc.   trilogy
10. <u>standing</u> still; not moving   stationary

2 Finish the sentences with the meaning of each word part. Use each meaning once. The word part is underlined to help you make the connection.

VOCABULARY LIST

many	two	one	first	stick
flow	most	stand	pouring	to carry

---

1. We have <u>bi</u>monthly meetings; it is good to get together and talk every __2__ months.

2. Currently in American society, <u>mono</u>gamy is the law. People seem to feel that it is better to have __1__ spouse at a time.

3. Anthony is <u>flu</u>ent in five languages. The ability to speak another language just seems to __flow__ out of him.

4. My great-grandfather was a <u>proto</u>martyr in the fight for safe working conditions for miners. In his town, he was the __first__ person to die in a riot caused by a strike.

5. Because I work for a <u>multi</u>national corporation, I could be transferred to __many__ countries.

6. Tina became confused at the meeting because people were __pouring__ out too many ideas at once.

7. The ad<u>hes</u>ive tape really helped my package __stick__ together. My sister said it took her an hour to get it open.

8. I reveal my inner<u>most</u> secrets to my diary. I don't dare share my __most__ secret feelings with anyone.

9. I asked the <u>port</u>er at the train station __to carry__ my bags to my car because I was tired of lifting them.

10. I am not going to let any ob<u>sta</u>cles (financial, emotional, or time-consuming) __stand__ in the way of my completing college.

---

3 Finish the story using the word parts found below. Use each word part once. Your knowledge of word parts, as well as the context clues, will help you create the correct words. If you do not understand the meaning of a word you have made, check the dictionary for the definition or to see whether the word exists.

WORD PARTS

ver	tri	plac	sti	bi
multi	most	flu	port	phobia

An Exciting Job

I work for a business that im__port__s furniture from around the world. The main offices are in New York and Los Angeles, so I have become __bi__costal with apartments in both cities. I am __tri__lingual: I speak English, Chinese, and Spanish. I am sent to several countries around the world. At first this was a problem for me because I suffered from aero~~phobia~~. I hated to fly. I overcame my fear because I wanted to enjoy the _____cultural aspect of my job. I love exploring many places. It is fascinating to see the in____ence countries have had on one another. The world is not a ___id place; changes are occurring everywhere. Some people are ob___nate and want time to stand still, but it won't. I am excited by the new things I see, and I am eager to check out the _____acity of a country's claim to have the biggest or best of anything. The northern_____ point I have been to is Hammerfest, Norway. It certainly was cold there, but I picked up some gorgeous tables and chairs.

4 Pick the best definition for each underlined word using your knowledge of word parts. Circle the word part in each of the underlined words.

a. always truthful

b. conduct; how one carries oneself

c. tending to unify or stick together

d. sweetly or smoothly flowing

e. not to be pacified or pleased

f. university with many campuses

g. stale or foul from standing, as in a pool of water

h. the action of a pouring out of anything

i. an abnormal fear of being alone

j. an original draft from which a document is prepared

_____ 1. Because our dog has <u>monophobia</u>, we have to take her with us everywhere.

_____ 2. Going to a <u>multiversity</u> can be tiring. I have to drive to four different campuses this semester to get to all my classes.

_____ 3. The secretary used the <u>protocol</u> to prepare the treaty for the next day's meeting.

_____ 4. I was proud of my son's <u>deportment</u> at the luncheon. He is usually loud, but he was quiet and well mannered.

_____ 5. The president had to face a <u>fusillade</u> of questions from reporters about his actions after it was discovered that he had been hiding money in a secret account.

_____ 6. My <u>veracious</u> sister has kept us from doing some wild things. I knew she would tell my parents if they asked why we were late.

_____ 7. The <u>stagnant</u> pond had a horrible smell to it.

_____ 8. The singer's <u>mellifluous</u> voice kept the audience enchanted for two hours.

_____ 9. Because of the movie's <u>cohesive</u> structure, it was easy to understand how the different characters all came to know each other.

_____ 10. The little boy was <u>implacable</u>; nothing would quiet him until his mother stopped at the toy store.

5 A good way to remember word parts is to pick one word that uses a word part and understand how that word part functions in the word. Then you can apply that meaning to other words that have the same word part. Use the words to help you match the word part to its meaning.

SET ONE

_____ 1. **bi-:** biannual, bicycle, binocular

_____ 2. **-flu-, -flux-:** fluid, influx, fluctuation

_____ 3. **-sta-, -sti-:** status, static, stationary

_____ 4. **-most:** utmost, foremost, southernmost

_____ 5. **-plac-:** placate, placid, placebo

a. to flow

b. to please

c. two

d. to stand, to be in a place

e. most

SET TWO

_____ 6. **multi-:** multitude, multiply, multilingual

_____ 7. **-fus-:** profuse, transfusion, infusion

_____ 8. **-ver-:** verify, verity, veracity

_____ 9. **-her-, -hes-:** coherent, inherent, adhesive

_____ 10. **-phobia:** acrophobia, metrophobia, numerophobia

f. fear of

g. to pour

h. many, much

i. truth

j. to stick

HINT

Campus Resources

Most colleges provide services to enhance your educational experience: learn to use these resources. Look into writing centers, computer labs, and tutoring programs for help as you prepare papers or study for tests. If you encounter any problems, consider the benefits of contacting counseling, disabled student services, or the financial aid office. You might also want to check into whether your campus offers any child-care facilities. Check your instructors' office hours and find their offices. Asking questions outside of class or getting help with papers during office hours are great ways to improve your learning. The faculty and staff on campus are there for you. Taking the time to find out where campus resources are located and what hours they are open can make your college experience more rewarding.

6 Use the dictionary to find a word you don't know that uses the word part. Write the meaning of the word part, the word, and the definition. If your dictionary has the etymology (history) of the word, see how the word part relates to the meaning, and write the etymology after the definition.

Word Part	Meaning	Word	Definition and Etymology
EXAMPLE:			
bi-	two	bicorn	having two horns or hornlike parts. Latin bicornis; bi- two + -corn having a horn
1. *sta-*			
2. *mono-*			
3. *port-*			
4. *ver-*			
5. *tri-*			

16 Literature

Look Deeply

HOST: Welcome to *Interviews with the Dead.* I know many of you suffer from **metrophobia**, but there is no reason to be afraid of poetry. Today my guests are two of the **foremost** poets of all time: Emily Dickinson and Robert "Bobby" Burns. Bobby, why don't you start us off by giving
5 an example of how you have used **similes**.

BOBBY: In my poem "A Red, Red Rose" I write:

> O My Luve's like a red, red rose,
>   That's newly sprung in June;
> O My Luve's like the melodie
10   That's sweetly played in tune.

The comparisons using *like* or *as* are similes. They are an effective way to get a reader to make a connection between two distinct things. I could have used a **metaphor** such as, "My luve is a rose." The direct comparison of an object with something that is usually not associated with it also helps the reader see
15 the object in a new way.

HOST: **Imagery** is certainly important to poetry. It is how we come to feel a poem.

BOBBY: That's right. Again in "A Red, Red Rose" I try to get the reader to use his or her senses to feel the speaker's love. In that first **stanza** I want the reader to see and smell the rose and hear the tune to understand the power of love.

20 HOST: Now, Emily, why is death such an important **motif** in your works? And why were all but two of your almost fifteen hundred poems published **posthumously**?

EMILY: I was a reclusive person, rarely seeing anyone most of my life. I didn't want attention, so it was better that my works were published after I died. Maybe my seclusion made me a bit morbid. But death is also a universal subject. In "Because I Could Not Stop for Death," I use
25 **personification** by giving death a carriage in which to pick up the speaker. Giving an inanimate object human characteristics can help a reader identify with the subject.

HOST: Why do you think people have such a hard time understanding poetry?

30 EMILY: Because people have to make **inferences** when they read poetry. Poets don't always come right out and tell the reader what they mean. The reader has to be willing to do some reasoning to figure out possible meanings. The interpreting can be one of the joys of reading poetry.

35 HOST: We've run out of time, but thank you both for helping my viewers to better understand poetry.

▌▌▌ PREDICTING

Cover the Word List below as you do the Predicting exercise. For each set, write the definition on the line next to the word to which it belongs. If you are unsure, return to the reading on page 82, and underline any context clues you find. After you've made your predictions, uncover the Word List and check your answers. Place a checkmark in the boxes next to the words whose definitions you missed. These are the words you'll want to study closely.

SET ONE

mental images   first in importance   a fear of poetry   a comparison using *like* or *as*
a comparison between things that are not literally alike

- ❑ 1. **metrophobia** (line 2) _____
- ❑ 2. **foremost** (line 3) _____
- ❑ 3. **simile** (line 5) _____
- ❑ 4. **metaphor** (line 13) _____
- ❑ 5. **imagery** (line 16) _____

SET TWO

the dominant theme in a work of art   the division of a poem   occurring after death
the act of giving inanimate objects human qualities   the act of drawing a conclusion

- ❑ 6. **stanza** (line 18) _____
- ❑ 7. **motif** (line 20) _____
- ❑ 8. **posthumously** (line 21) _____
- ❑ 9. **personification** (line 25) _____
- ❑ 10. **inference** (line 30) _____

▌▌▌ WORD LIST

foremost
[fôr′ mōst]
adj. first in importance, place, or time; chief

imagery
[im′ ij rē]
n. 1. the use of vivid descriptions to make mental images or pictures
2. mental images

inference
[in′ fər əns]
n. the act of drawing a conclusion from evidence

metaphor
[met′ ə fôr′, fər]
n. a figure of speech that makes a comparison between things that are not literally alike

metrophobia
[me ′ trə fo′ bē ə, mē]
n. a fear of poetry

motif
[mō tēf′]
n. the dominant theme in a literary or musical composition; a recurring element in a work of art

personification
[pər son′ ə fi kā′ shən]
n. 1. the act of giving human qualities to inanimate objects or abstract ideas
2. a person or thing that is the perfect example of a quality; an embodiment

posthumously
[pos′ choo məs lē]
adv. 1. occurring after death
2. published after the death of the author

simile
[sim ′ ə lē]
n. a figure of speech that compares two unlike things, introduced by the words *like* or *as*

stanza
[stan′ zə]
n. a group of lines of poetry having a definite pattern; the division of a poem

© 2005 Pearson Education, Inc.

1 Circle the correct meaning of each vocabulary word.

1. posthumously: occurring before birth   occurring after death

2. imagery: mental images   real items

3. metrophobia: a love of poetry   a fear of poetry

4. metaphor: a comparison using *like* or *as*   a direct comparison

5. stanza: the division of a poem   the first line of a poem

6. inference: making a wild guess   drawing a conclusion from evidence

7. foremost: least   leading

8. personification: a person without any good qualities   a person that is the perfect example of a quality

9. motif: a recurring element   an element used once

10. simile: a comparison using *like* or *as*   a direct comparison

2 Match each word to the appropriate example.

VOCABULARY LIST

| foremost | simile | imagery | stanza | metrophobia |
| inference | motifs | metaphor | posthumously | personification |

1. His smile is a bolt of lightning. _metaphor_
2. Her first novel was printed fifty years after her death. _posthumously_
3. "I'm afraid to read Whitman's poem *Leaves of Grass*." _metrophobia_
4. The tree's branches spread over me like a fortress. _simile_
5. The walls shook with laughter, the ceiling had a wide grin, and the floors just smiled; the house knew my cleaning wouldn't last a day. _pers._
6. I bit into the large, cream-cheese frosted, freshly baked cinnamon roll; listened to the screams from the midway rides; and felt the warm sun on my back—it was good to be at the county fair. _stanza imagery_

7. Yesterday was the change to daylight saving time, and John is an hour late; he probably didn't change his clock. _inference_

8. Nature's beauty, lost love, and patriotism are a few common ones. _motifs_

9. Water, water, everywhere,
   And all the boards did shrink;
   Water, water, everywhere,
   Nor any drop to drink. _stanza_

10. William Shakespeare as a playwright and poet, and Beethoven in music. _foremost_

3 Finish the sentences using the vocabulary words. Use each word once.

VOCABULARY LIST

metrophobia	stanza	imagery	simile	foremost
personification	metaphor	motif	inference	posthumously

1. Kafka didn't want his writing published _posthumously_, so he asked his friend to destroy all of his remaining work.

2. Time is an important _motif_ in many of Edgar Allan Poe's works.

3. The last _stanza_ of Edwin Arlington Robinson's "Richard Cory" tells the reader the surprising twist to Cory's supposed good life.

4. In "A Birthday" Christina Rossetti writes, "My heart is like an apple tree / Whose boughs are bent with thick set fruit." The _simile_ shows how happy the speaker is because she has found love.

5. My friend compared himself to a battleship. That _metaphor_ fits him because he loves conflict.

6. Robert Frost is one of the _foremost_ American poets.

7. William Carlos Williams uses _imagery_ to help the reader see the wheelbarrow. He describes it as being red and "glazed with rain / water / beside the white / chickens."

8. *The Wonderful Wizard of Oz* uses _per m_ when the tree yells at Dorothy for picking one of its apples.

9. When the woman in the story said her husband wouldn't be coming to dinner, the reader had to make a(n) _inference_ because no direct reason for his disappearance was given.

10. Because some poets use many historical and literary references, their poems can be hard to understand, which has led to _metrophobia_ for many people.

Write a poem about love or death using four of the following elements: imagery, metaphor, motif, personification, simile, or stanza. Don't let metrophobia get in the way. You don't have to write a great poem; this is just a chance to practice using the vocabulary words.

_____

_____

_____

_____

_____

_____

_____

_____

_____

_____

_____

_____

_____

17 Art History

The European Gallery

Joseph Turner
British 1775–1851
Burning of the Houses of Parliament
watercolor 1843

5 Turner captures the **essence** of the fire through the various **hues**. The red, orange, and yellow colors convey the heat of the fire, while the darker colors are **evocative** of the smoke. The whole painting is **emblematic** of the fire without directly showing it.

Joseph Mallord William Turner, *Burning of the Houses of Parliament*, 1843. Watercolor. Copyright Clore Collection, Tate Gallery, London/Art Resource, NY

10 El Greco (Doménikos Theotokópoulos)
Spanish (b. Crete) 1541–1613
View and Map of Toledo
oil on canvas c. 1613–1620

El Greco's limited color **spectrum** gives the painting a
15 somewhat somber quality. The severity of the scene, however, is offset by his use of **perspective** that causes the eye to move from the foreground figures to the Virgin and angels in the sky. The dramatic clouds and floating figures give energy to what could be consid-
20 ered an **austere** painting.

El Greco (Domenikos Theotokópoulos) (1541–1613), *View and Map of Toledo*. Canvas, 132 × 228 cm. Casa y Museo del Greco, Toledo, Spain. Copyright Erich Lessing/Art Resource, NY

Vincent van Gogh
Dutch 1853–1890
Yellow Wheat and Cypresses
oil on canvas 1889

25 Van Gogh uses several colors in his **palette** to express the grandeur of nature. This **picturesque** scene draws the viewer into his multicolored, swirling world. **Eschewing** conventional techniques, van Gogh uses thick brush strokes to make his scenes come alive.

Vincent van Gogh (1853–1890), *Yellow Wheat and Cypresses*, 1889. Oil on canvas. National Gallery, London, Great Britain. Copyright Erich Lessing/Art Resource, NY

▋▋▋ PREDICTING

Cover the Word List below as you do the Predicting exercise. For each set, write the definition on the line next to the word to which it belongs. If you are unsure, return to the reading on page 87, and underline any context clues you find. After you've made your predictions, uncover the Word List and check your answers. Place a checkmark in the boxes next to the words whose definitions you missed. These are the words you'll want to study closely.

SET ONE

symbolic   color   the crucial element   a range of related qualities   suggestive

❑   1.   **essence** (line 5) _____

❑   2.   **hue** (line 6) _____

❑   3.   **evocative** (line 8) _____

❑   4.   **emblematic** (line 9) _____

❑   5.   **spectrum** (line 14) _____

SET TWO

charming   to avoid   severe   range of colors used in a painting
techniques for representing three-dimensional objects on a two-dimensional surface

❑   6.   **perspective** (line 16) _____

❑   7.   **austere** (line 20) _____

❑   8.   **palette** (line 25) _____

❑   9.   **picturesque** (line 26) _____

❑   10.   **eschew** (line 27) _____

▋▋▋ WORD LIST

austere   *adj.*   1. severe or stern; somber
[ô stîr']   2. simple; bare

emblematic   *adj.*   serving as an emblem;
[em' blə mat' ik]   symbolic; representative

eschew   *v.*   to avoid; to shun; to escape
[es chōo']

essence   *n.*   1. the quality of a thing that
[es' əns]   gives it its identity; the crucial
                             element; core

evocative   *adj.*   having the power to call forth
[i vok' ə tiv]   or produce a reaction;
                             suggestive

hue   *n.*   1. color
[hyōo]   2. a particular gradation of
                             color; tint; shade
                             3. character; aspect

palette   *n.*   1. the range of colors used
[pal' it]   in a particular painting or by
                             a particular artist
                             2. a board, typically with a
                             hole for the thumb, upon
                             which an artist mixes colors

perspective   *n.*   1. any of various techniques for
[pər spek' tiv]   representing three-dimensional
                             objects and depth relationships
                             on a two-dimensional surface
                             2. a view
                             3. a point of view; attitude

picturesque   *adj.*   1. charming; interesting in an
[pik' chə resk']   unusual way; vivid
                             2. suitable for a picture

spectrum   *n.*   a range of related qualities,
[spek' trəm]   ideas, or activities; variety

sombre
Темный
похмурен.

1 Put a T for true or F for false next to each sentence.

_____ 1. Pink is an austere color.

_____ 2. A painting of garbage cans would probably be referred to as *picturesque.*

_____ 3. A person's perspective can change when he or she is given more information.

_____ 4. Flags are emblematic of a country.

_____ 5. Bell-bottom pants are evocative of the 1960s.

_____ 6. Most people would eschew the offer of a free plane ticket.

_____ 7. The essence of doing well in school is studying.

_____ 8. An artist's palette usually contains only black, white, and gray.

_____ 9. Most people like a spectrum of activities to choose from when on vacation.

_____ 10. A popular hue for buildings is lime green.

2 In each group, circle the word that does not have a connection to the other three words. See Chapter 3 for an example.

1. symbolic	direct	emblematic	representative
2. edge	spirit	essence	core
3. hue	color	tint	bare
4. variety	range	sameness	spectrum
5. palette	board	range	singular
6. eschew	avoid	escape	join
7. elaborate	austere	stern	simple
8. vivid	charming	ugly	picturesque
9. view	indifferent	perspective	attitude
10. evocative	suggestive	summon	stated

3 Complete the following quotations overheard in art museums around the world. Use each word once.

1. "Rembrandt's paintings are too ___austere___ for me; the man needs to lighten up."

2. "In her glorious flower paintings, O'Keeffe effectively uses her ___palette___ to present the rich colors of nature."

3. "Diego Rivera's mural gave me a better ___per___ on the struggles in Mexico."

4. "I like the ___hues___ quality of Georges Seurat's *Sunday Afternoon on the Island of La Grande Jatte.* The pointillist technique and the colors make it an interesting and charming work."

5. "I know Picasso was trying to _____ traditional forms in his paintings, but I cannot see a woman coming down that staircase."

6. "The African mask exhibit was _____ of how we often hide who we are."

7. "Dali's paintings really capture the _____ of the dreamworld."

8. "The pink and purple ___hues___ in Suzanne Valadon's *Lilacs and Peonies* show the delicacy of spring."

9. "I appreciate the ___spectrum___ of works in the modern art section; there is everything from a Warhol painting to a huge plastic banana."

10. "I found the Hiroshige print of the rain shower to be quite ___evocative___; I could feel myself in a downpour."

Georgia O'Keeffe (1887–1986), *White Flower on Red Earth, #1,* 1943. Oil on canvas, 26 in. × 30 1/4 in. Collection of the Newark Museum, Newark, New Jersey. Copyright The Newark Museum/Art Resource, NY. © 2002 The Georgia O'Keeffe Foundation/Artists Rights Society (ARS), New York

VOCABULARY LIST

emblematic

essence

hues

perspective

spectrum

austere

eschew

evocative

palette

picturesque

Georges Seurat (French, 1859–1891), *A Sunday on La Grande Jatte,* 1884–86. Oil on canvas, 207.6 × 308 cm. Helen Birch Bartlett Memorial Collection, The Art Institute of Chicago. 1926.224. Photograph © 2001, The Art Institute of Chicago. All Rights Reserved.

HINT

Make It Yours

An important step in learning new vocabulary is to practice using the words. When you feel comfortable with a word's definition, start using the word in your writing and conversations. If you only try to memorize the word for a test, you will likely forget it after the test. Make your acquisition of new vocabulary meaningful by using the words in everyday situations. Also try to connect the word to prior knowledge or experiences. Are there situations you have been in in which the word would be appropriate? Try to integrate the word with your life as much as possible. You will impress your friends and family and feel good about yourself as you show people what you have learned.

▮▮▮ INTERACTIVE EXERCISE

You are an art critic. Use seven of the vocabulary words to write a column about Claude Monet's painting *White Waterlilies*.

_____
_____
_____
_____
_____
_____
_____
_____
_____
_____
_____
_____
_____

Claude Monet (1840–1926), *White Waterlilies,* Pushkin Museum of Fine Arts, Moscow. Copyright Scala/Art Resource, NY

_____
_____
_____
_____
_____
_____
_____
_____

18 Foreign Languages

Creeping into English

More foreign words and phrases creep into common English usage each year. Because English has always borrowed words from other languages, people aren't always aware that a word originated in another country. For example, banana and zombie are African words, cookie and yacht come from the Dutch, and yogurt from Turkish. Other words still sound foreign, but they are used everyday when
5 speaking English.

Imagine eating dinner **alfresco** on a pleasant evening. While you are enjoying the outdoors, your waiter comes to tell you about the soup **du jour** and other daily specials. After you take a sip of the delicious French onion soup you ordered, you sit back and enjoy a **bon mot** your companion has just uttered. As you smile at his witty remark, you think, "I'm living **la dolce vita** as I take pleasure in my
10 excellent meal, good company, and lovely atmosphere." **Voilà!** Possibly without even being aware of it, you have just spent an evening relying on foreign phrases.

Foreign words also appear frequently in the media. The Latin phrase **carpe diem** was an important message in the film *Dead Poet's Society,* and the words appear on numerous calendars and motivational posters. To seize the day is a message we often forget in today's hectic world. The term
15 **doppelgänger** comes from German for a ghostly double, and the concept has been explored in works by writers such as Edgar Allan Poe and Robert Louis Stevenson. Even a single word can have an impact in a story, such as **nada** as used in "A Clean Well-Lighted Place" by Ernest Hemingway. Nothing can certainly come to mean something.

It isn't necessarily a **faux pas** to not understand every foreign word or phrase currently in use, but
20 to avoid possibly embarrassing moments the wise person will want to learn these phrases. The multicultural **zeitgeist** of the twenty-first century asks all of us to grow along with the language.

▮▮▮ PREDICTING

Cover the Word List below as you do the Predicting exercise. For each set, write the definition on the line next to the word to which it belongs. If you are unsure, return to the reading on page 92, and underline any context clues you find. After you've made your predictions, uncover the Word List and check your answers. Place a checkmark in the boxes next to the words whose definitions you missed. These are the words you'll want to study closely.

SET ONE

There it is!   a witty remark   out-of-doors   the good life
as served on a particular day

❑ 1. **alfresco** (line 6) _____

❑ 2. **du jour** (line 7) _____

❑ 3. **bon mot** (line 8) _____

❑ 4. **la dolce vita** (line 9) _____

❑ 5. **voilà** (line 10) _____

SET TWO

nothing   the spirit of the time   seize the day   a mistake
a ghostly double or counterpart

❑ 6. **carpe diem** (line 12) _____

❑ 7. **doppelgänger** (line 15) _____

❑ 8. **nada** (line 17) _____

❑ 9. **faux pas** (line 19) _____

❑ 10. **zeitgeist** (line 21) _____

▮▮▮ WORD LIST

alfresco
[al fres′ kō]
Italian. *adv.* out-of-doors; in the open air
adj. outdoor

bon mot
[bôn mō′]
French. *n.* a witty remark or comment; witticism

carpe diem
[kär′ pē di′ əm, kär′ pā dē′ əm]
Latin. *n.* seize the day; enjoy the present

dolce vita
[dôl′ che vē′tä]
Italian. *n.* the good life (usually preceded by *la*)

doppelgänger
[dop′ əl gang′ ər]
German. *n.* a ghostly double or counterpart of a living person

du jour
[də zhoor′, dōo]
French. *adj.* 1. as prepared or served on a particular day
2. fashionable; current

faux pas
[fō pä′]
French. *n.* a mistake; a slip or blunder in manners or conduct; an embarrassing social error

nada
[nä′ dä]
Spanish. *n.* nothing

voilà
[vwä lä′]
French. *interj.* There it is! (used to express success or satisfaction)

zeitgeist
[tsīt′ gīst′]
German. *n.* the spirit of the time; the general feeling of a particular period of time

1 Match each word with its synonym in Set One and its antonym in Set Two.

SYNONYMS

SET ONE

_____ 1. carpe diem   a. mood

_____ 2. doppelgänger   b. mistake

_____ 3. bon mot   c. grab the chance

_____ 4. zeitgeist   d. double

_____ 5. faux pas   e. witticism

ANTONYMS

SET TWO

_____ 6. alfresco   f. old

_____ 7. nada   g. Darn!

_____ 8. la dolce vita   h. indoors

_____ 9. voilà   i. everything

_____ 10. du jour   j. dullness

2 Finish the sentences using the vocabulary words. Use each word once.

VOCABULARY LIST

bon mot	nada	alfresco	dolce vita	doppelgänger
carpe diem	voilà	faux pas	zeitgeist	du jour

1. The special _du jour_ at the cafeteria was kidney pie; I decided to pass.
2. As we sat on the porch of our cabin overlooking the lake, we thought this was the _la dolce vita_.
3. Edgar Allan Poe has a scary story about a man who meets his _doppelgänger_ at a party.
4. My cousin is the expert at the _faux pas_ _bon mot_; she always knows the right thing to say to make people laugh.
5. After a busy semester, I was looking forward to doing _carpe diem_ _nada_ for a week.
6. Sometimes I get so involved in everything I need to get done that I forget to _carpe diem_.
7. I think that having toilet paper stuck to one's shoe all night would be considered a(n) _faux pas_ at most parties.
8. In the 1920s the _zeitgeist_ seemed to be to party as much as possible in order to forget World War I.
9. The play will be performed _alfresco_ to enhance the play's forest setting.
10. I kept trying, and, _voilà_, my story was finally accepted for publication.

3 Connect the vocabulary words to the following items or situations. Use each word once.

VOCABULARY LIST

alfresco	carpe diem	du jour	doppelgänger	voilà
bon mot	faux pas	la dolce vita	nada	zeitgeist

1. a pocket without any lira, pesos, or francs _nada_
2. French onion soup _du jour_
3. greed in the 1980s _zeitgeist_
4. under the stars _alfresco_
5. "There is only one thing in the world worse than being talked about, and that is not being talked about."—Oscar Wilde _bon mot_
6. I found my keys! _voilà_
7. asking a woman whether her child is her grandchild _faux pas_
8. When the woman he has admired all semester asks to borrow a pen, the young man asks her out. _la dolce vita_
9. Robert Louis Stevenson's character Markheim meets his evil self. _doppelgänger_
10. a three-course lunch followed by a nap _carpe diem_

▌▌▌ INTERACTIVE EXERCISE

Pretend you have enrolled in a Semester Abroad program, and write a letter to a friend telling about your adventures overseas. Use at least seven of the vocabulary words in your note.

_____
_____
_____
_____
_____
_____
_____
_____
_____
_____
_____
_____
_____

19 Biology

A Walk in the Woods

Welcome to the Small Woods Nature Trail!

By using this guide you will learn about the **flora** and **fauna** of the area. A variety of plants and animals live in the woods and interact with each other in order to survive. Look for the numbered signposts that correspond with this guide. Enjoy your **sojourn** through the **myriad** wonders of nature!

Stop 1 In front of you is an example of a **parasitic** relationship. The mistletoe plant has attached itself to the oak tree and is using the moisture and food from the tree to feed itself. Sometimes the mistletoe can get so large that it ends up killing its host. [5]

If you are here in the autumn, you will also see that the oak is losing its leaves. Most oak trees are **deciduous**, meaning they lose their leaves in the fall. You may not remember it, but you also had a deciduous part in your body. Baby teeth are called deciduous teeth because they fall out as a part of the growing process. [10]

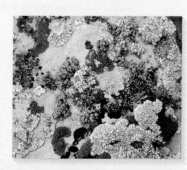

Stop 2 In contrast to the parasitic relationship of the mistletoe and the oak tree, here you see a **symbiotic** relationship in the **lichen** growing on the rocks at your feet. Lichen are plants made up of a fungus and an alga growing together. The fungi use the food made by the algae and the algae use the water absorbed by the fungi. The two materials help each other survive. Lichen grow on rocks and trees, and about sixteen thousand **species** have been identified. Some types of lichen are used as food by animals such as reindeer in the arctic areas and even by humans. Lichens are also used in making perfumes. As you continue your walk, look for the various colors of lichen from gray to green to white. When they are moist, the lichen are usually a bright green. [15] [20] [25]

Stop 3 The pine trees around you are examples of evergreens. Unlike deciduous trees, the leaves of evergreens stay green all year.

Stop 4 At the right time of year, you can enjoy the beauty of butterflies fluttering around you. Butterflies go through a four-stage **metamorphosis**. They go from egg to larva (a caterpillar) to pupa (the resting stage) to adult. The colorful butterflies you see are in the adult stage. Butterflies are useful to the woods as they often pollinate flowers. [30]

▌▌▌ PREDICTING

Cover the Word List below as you do the Predicting exercise. For each set, write the definition on the line next to the word to which it belongs. If you are unsure, return to the reading on page 96, and underline any context clues you find. After you've made your predictions, uncover the Word List and check your answers. Place a checkmark in the boxes next to the words whose definitions you missed. These are the words you'll want to study closely.

SET ONE

a temporary stay   living off another species   animals   plants   innumerable

- ❑ 1. **flora** (line 2) _____
- ❑ 2. **fauna** (line 2) _____
- ❑ 3. **sojourn** (line 4) _____
- ❑ 4. **myriad** (line 4) _____
- ❑ 5. **parasitic** (line 5) _____

SET TWO

a change in form   shedding the leaves annually   organisms having common qualities
a beneficial relationship   an organism composed of a fungus and an alga

- ❑ 6. **deciduous** (line 10) _____
- ❑ 7. **symbiotic** (line 15) _____
- ❑ 8. **lichen** (line 15) _____
- ❑ 9. **species** (line 20) _____
- ❑ 10. **metamorphosis** (line 30) _____

▌▌▌ WORD LIST

deciduous
[di sij ′ o͞o əs]
adj. 1. shedding the leaves annually, as certain trees do 2. falling off at a particular stage of growth; transitory

fauna
[fô ′ nə]
n. the animals of a given region or period taken as a whole

flora
[flôr ′ ə, flōr ′ ə]
n. the plants of a given region or period taken as a whole

lichen
[lī ′ kən]
n. a complex organism composed of a fungus in symbiotic union with an alga, commonly forming patches on rocks and trees

metamorphosis
[met′ ə môr ′ fə sis]
n. 1. a change in form from one stage to the next in the life of an organism 2. a transformation

myriad
[mir ′ ē ad]
adj. of an indefinitely great number; innumerable
n. an immense number

parasitic
[par′ ə sit ′ ik]
adj. pertaining to a parasite (1. an organism that lives on another species without aiding the host; 2. a person who takes advantage of others)

sojourn
[n. sō′ jûrn]
[v. sō jûrn′]
n. a temporary stay
v. to stay temporarily

species
[spē′ shēz, sēz]
n. organisms having some common qualities; kind or type

symbiotic
[sim bē ot′ ik]
adj. 1. pertaining to symbiosis—the living together of two dissimilar organisms
2. any mutually beneficial relationship between two persons or groups

1 Circle the word that best completes each sentence.

1. My (sojourn, myriad) in the Amazon only lasted five weeks, but I loved every minute of it.

2. After just three days of kindergarten, the child's (species, metamorphosis) from being extremely afraid to feeling confident was amazing.

3. The (fauna, flora) in the desert, from the brittle bush to the ocotillo plant, really bloom in the spring after a shower.

4. There were (parasitic, myriad) reasons why I was unable to make the meeting. I can't even start to tell you the problems I ran into that day.

5. The roommates' relationship became quite (symbiotic, parasitic) as they helped each other with homework and chores based on their strengths.

6. The (fauna, flora) in the woods include small animals such as squirrels and bigger animals like dear.

7. The (lichen, sojourn) covered the rocks and trees throughout the forest.

8. I think the autumn is a lovely time of year because the (parasitic, deciduous) trees in our neighborhood turn beautiful colors.

9. My friendship with Joanne started out well, but it has become (symbiotic, parasitic); all she does now is ask me for money and favors.

10. There are several (species, flora) of birds in the marsh, so we should have a great time bird watching this morning.

2 Match each item to the vocabulary word it best relates to. Use each word once.

VOCABULARY LIST

fauna	deciduous	lichen	flora	myriad
symbiotic	species	sojourn	parasitic	metamorphosis

1. pebbles on a beach, stars in the sky _myriad_

2. ivy, roses _flora_

3. the homely girl in most teenage movies, moths _metamorphosis_

4. at the beach, to the mountains _sojourn_

5. maple trees, a stag's horns _deciduous_

6. fox, squirrel _fauna_

7. on rocks, on the sides of trees _lichen_

8. the wood lily, the meadow lily _species_

9. an unemployed relative who comes to stay and ends up watching television all day, fleas and ticks _parasitic_

10. the hermit crab and sea anemone, the white cattle egret and the elephant _symbiotic_

3 Finish the journal entries using the vocabulary words. Use each word once.

SET ONE

VOCABULARY LIST

lichen	species	myriad	deciduous	flora

October 29, 2004

My early morning hike in the forest was wonderful. The air was crisp, and wispy clouds blew across the sky. The (1) _deciduous_ trees are beginning to lose their leaves. Red, gold, and brown leaves carpeted the ground. The (2) _____ were a bright green in the morning mist. All of the (3) _flora_ had a magical quality to it: the flowers danced and the trees whispered to me. Every (4) _species_ of plant seemed to have some advice, from the oak telling me to be strong to the dandelion urging me to go where the wind takes me. A (5) _myriad_ of possibilities opened before me as I strolled through nature's majesty.

SET TWO

VOCABULARY LIST

metamorphosis	fauna	sojourn	parasitic	symbiotic

April 2, 2005

Today the first buds of spring are appearing on many of the trees. I am so lucky to be able to see the (6) _metamorphosis_ of the forest. I also spied a deer during my (7) _sojourn_. Of all the (8) _fauna_ in the forest, the deer are my favorite. They are such beautiful creatures. I have always been afraid that my relationship with nature has been a (9) _parasitic_ one. I get so much enjoyment from plants and animals, but have never felt that I have been able to give anything in return. Yesterday circumstances changed. I signed up to be a docent, and now the relationship can be (10) _symbiotic_. I can still find peace from the forest, but I can also help to protect it by educating people about the joys of nature.

INTERACTIVE EXERCISE

Your biology class has just taken the walk through Small Woods. Your instructor has given you the following worksheet to complete.

Name _____

1. List two types of fauna and two types of flora that you saw.

   _____ _____ , _____ _____

2. Did you see any deciduous trees? How could you tell?

   _____

3. What color lichen did you see? Where did you spot the lichen?

   _____   _____

4. Name two species you saw.

   _____   _____

5. What stage of metamorphosis were the butterflies in?

   _____

6. Describe how humans have had a parasitic relationship with nature. What can we do to make our relationship with nature more symbiotic?

   _____

   _____

7. Although we do have a myriad of choices of places for field trips, where do you suggest our next sojourn take us?

   _____

Focus on Chapters 11–19

1. _____ v

2. _____ 0

3. _____ affluence

4. _____ al

5. _____ hues

6. _____ monolith

7. _____ pa

8. _____ enclave

9. _____ lichen

10. _____ multitude

11. _____ p

12. _____ p

The following activities give you a chance to interact some more with the vocabulary words you've been learning. By looking at art, acting, writing, taking tests, and doing a crossword puzzle, you will see which words you know well and which you still need to work with.

ART

Match each picture on page 101 to one of the following vocabulary words. Use each word once.

VOCABULARY LIST

alfresco	visualization	oasis	personification
palette	lichen	multitude	affluence
enclave	portfolio	hues	monolith

DRAMA

Charades: You will be given one of the following words to act out in class. Think about how this word could be demonstrated without speaking. The other people in class will try to guess what word you are showing.

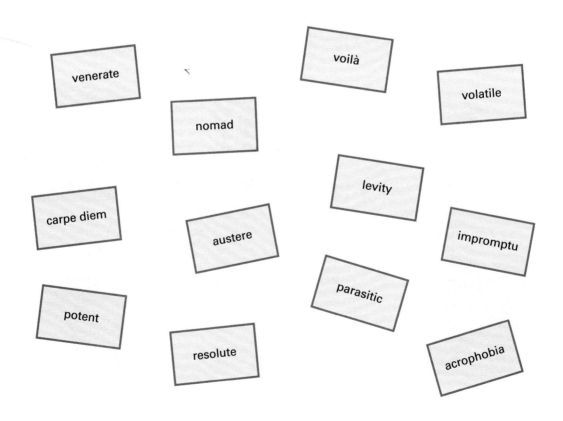

venerate

voilà

volatile

nomad

levity

carpe diem

austere

impromptu

potent

parasitic

resolute

acrophobia

Answer the following questions to further test your understanding of the vocabulary words.

1. What country's hinterland would you like to explore? Why?

   _____

2. If someone was making derogatory statements about a good friend of yours, what would you say to the person?

   _____

3. Write an anecdote about a friend or family member.

   _____

   _____

4. How can someone overcome metrophobia?

   _____

   _____

5. Name two ways a monopoly might be broken.

   _____

   _____

6. What kind of terrain do you enjoy walking on? _____

7. Where would you like to sojourn during the summer?

   _____

8. What is the foremost problem at your college? What is a possible solution?

   _____

   _____

9. What could change a person's perspective about a topic?

   _____

10. Give two examples of *la dolce vita*.

    _____

    _____

11. Name two types of fauna that you like.

    _____   _____

12. In the spectrum of team sports, what two are your favorites to watch or play?

    _____   _____

1 Finish the story using the vocabulary words. Use each word once.

VOCABULARY LIST

equity	fortitude	myriad	ramifications	successive
essence	inference	procure	ravine	wane
faux pas	mutual			

The Vacation That Never Happened

My simple vacation became an adventure I would like to forget. Our plan was to go camping in the mountains, about five hours away. For a (1) _multitude_ of reasons, we never quite made it. I thought, by (2) _____ agreement, that my friend and I were going to take Friday off to avoid the week-end traffic. However, when I got to his house, he wasn't there. The obvious (3) _____ was that he had gone to work, so I called, and there he was. I asked him what had happened, but there wasn't much coherence in his reply. First he gave me one reason and then another. I told him to forget it and just get to my house. Then we had to make (4) _____ stops to get items I thought Tom would have already had. He still had to (5) _____ his part of the groceries, reclaim his sleeping bag from the dry cleaners, and buy a book to read. My enthusiasm for this trip was already starting to (6) _____.

Finally, we left town, but the (7) _____ of these delays became apparent as we hit the freeway. We ended up sitting in traffic for over an hour. After being in the driver's seat for four hours, I was ready for Tom to take over. However, he said he didn't feel like driving. I didn't think I was be-ing unreasonable. All I was asking for was some (8) _____. At last we made it to the camp-

ground, and that was when I needed all my (9) _____ to keep from breaking down or killing Tom. He hadn't made the reservations, and there was no room for us. Then Tom said it was my (10) _____ for trusting him to make the reservations. At that point, there was a (11) _____ that looked mighty inviting to throw him into. The (12) _____ of our friendship remains intact because basically Tom is a fun guy, but I'll think hard before I take another va-cation with him.

2 Pick the word that best completes each sentence.

1. I need to make an appointment for my _____ checkup with the dentist.

   a. profuse   b. biannual   c. potent   d. derogatory

2. The _____ that best fits the atmosphere of my math class is that it's like being in a grave.

   a. simile   b. nada   c. enclave   d. monolith

3. The speaker's _____ gave me a chance to see whether I had written down all the major points he had made.

   a. zeitgeist   b. monopoly   c. escapade   d. summation

4. The _____ of my hometown on the news wasn't very flattering; I never thought of it as being filled with trash and toxic waste.

   a. nomad   b. portfolio   c. depiction   d. testimony

5. On our last trip we discovered that several countries _____ an airport departure tax.

   a. levy   b. procure   c. wane   d. venerate

6. Because my grandmother is saving her doll collection for _____, I wasn't allowed to play with the dolls when I was little.

   a. imagery   b. posterity   c. summation   d. essence

7. Karl amused his dinner companions with a _____ about the waiter's service.

   a. motif   b. spectrum   c. fauna   d. bon mot

8. Sometimes it can be hard to find material that is _____ to one's argument, but for a good paper the writer must keep searching.

   a. mutual   b. relevant   c. profuse   d. impromptu

9. In biology we learned about _____ relationships among animals; I was amazed at the different ways species help each other.

   a. austere   b. alfresco   c. symbiotic   d. picturesque

10. The argument at the luncheon was _____ of all the problems the department is experiencing without strong leadership.

    a. parasitic   b. foremost   c. du jour   d. emblematic

11. When my friend came to dinner, I wondered what the crisis _____ would be; she was never without a problem.

    a. symbiotic   b. du jour   c. profuse   d. derogatory

12. During the spring the _____ in the park is especially beautiful.

    a. flora   b. imagery   c. essence   d. testimony

Use the following words to complete the crossword puzzle. You will use each word once.

VOCABULARY LIST

deciduous	nada
doppelgänger	picturesque
escapade	posthumously
eschew	profuse
evocative	species
fluctuation	stanza
imagery	testimony
metamorphosis	topography
metaphor	verity
motif	zeitgeist

Across
2. suggestive
4. the division of a poem
7. a change in form
11. to escape
16. charming; vivid
18. an irregular variation
19. a ghostly double
20. mental pictures

Down
1. the spirit of the time
3. evidence in support of a fact
5. the detailed description of an area
6. occurring after death
8. a kind or type
9. With trees, note this quality in autumn
10. The moon is a crystal ball.
12. the dominant theme
13. extravagant
14. the quality of being real
15. a reckless adventure
17. nothing

A Healthy Dose of News

Health Watch

Your source for health and lifestyle tips

Do Herbal Medicines Work?

Consumers should be **wary**, as studies are still inconclusive for many herbal medicines. What is often working is the **placebo** effect. Because people believe a drug is effective, they feel better. A few herbs such as echinacea appear to be helpful if used for a short time. Some studies show that echinacea may lessen the duration of colds and flu, but it probably doesn't prevent either.

If you take herbal supplements, make sure you get them from a **bona fide** vitamin company. The Food and Drug Administration does not regulate herbal supplements, so shop carefully.

When to Worry About Forgetfulness

Dementia is a **dysfunction** that more people are becoming concerned about. Dementia is a deterioration in mental and social skills that is serious enough to have an influence on one's everyday activities. Dementia comes in several forms including Alzheimer's disease. You shouldn't be **paranoid** and think you are suffering from dementia if you forget where you put your car keys once or twice a month, but extreme forgetfulness can be a symptom. If you have any **qualms** about your or a loved one's mental health, talk to a physician to help determine whether the problem is serious or what may be causing the problem.

Quick Tips

Not every spot means cancer, and not every cancer is **malignant**. Some cancers can be cured. See your doctor about any unusual spots or moles or if you notice a change in a spot or mole.

Whenever you suspect a health problem, contact your doctor. With a proper examination, you can both decide whether the problem is **inconsequential**. If it bothers you, you should discuss the matter with your physician. If the problem is **perennial**, don't ignore it. Any enduring or recurring ailments should be examined.

▮▮▮ PREDICTING

Cover the Word List below as you do the Predicting exercise. For each set, write the definition on the line next to the word to which it belongs. If you are unsure, return to the reading on page 107, and underline any context clues you find. After you've made your predictions, uncover the Word List and check your answers. Place a checkmark in the boxes next to the words whose definitions you missed. These are the words you'll want to study closely.

SET ONE

genuine   disordered performance of a bodily system   cautious
a deterioration of intellectual abilities   a substance without medicine

❑ 1. **wary** (line 4) _____

❑ 2. **placebo** (line 6) _____

❑ 3. **bona fide** (line 19) _____

❑ 4. **dementia** (line 25) _____

❑ 5. **dysfunction** (line 25) _____

SET TWO

threatening to life or health   everlasting   showing abnormal distrust
feelings of doubt   lacking importance

❑ 6. **paranoid** (line 33) _____

❑ 7. **qualms** (line 38) _____

❑ 8. **malignant** (line 43) _____

❑ 9. **inconsequential** (line 47) _____

❑ 10. **perennial** (line 49) _____

▮▮▮ WORD LIST

bona fide
[bō' nə fid']
adj. 1. genuine
2. done or made in good faith; sincere

dementia
[di men' shə, shē ə]
n. a deterioration of intellectual abilities along with emotional disturbances due to a brain disorder; madness

dysfunction
[dis fungk' shən]
n. disordered or impaired performance of a bodily system or organ

inconsequential
[in kon' sə kwen' shəl]
adj. 1. lacking importance; petty
2. illogical; irrelevant
n. a triviality

malignant
[mə lig' nənt]
adj. 1. threatening to life or health
2. evil in nature

paranoid
[par' ə noid']
adj. showing unreasonable or abnormal distrust or suspicion
n. one afflicted with paranoia

perennial
[pə ren' ē əl]
adj. 1. lasting through the year or through many years; everlasting
2. continually recurring

placebo
[plə sē' bō]
n. 1. a substance without medicine given to humor a patient
2. an inactive substance used as a control in an experiment
3. anything lacking real value; done or given to humor another

qualm
[kwäm, kwôm]
n. 1. a feeling of doubt or misgiving; uneasiness
2. a sudden feeling of sickness, faintness, or nausea

wary
[wâr' ē]
adj. cautious; watchful

▮▮▮▮ SELF-TESTS

1 Put a T for true or F for false next to each statement.

_____ **T** 1. People should be wary of offers sent to their e-mail from companies or people they don't know.

unimp   inconsequential

_____ 2. A gas leak is an inconsequential problem.

_____ 3. Feeling paranoid makes it easy to cope with life.

_____ **F** 4. Dealing with a teenager's desire for increased freedom has been a perennial problem for most parents.

_____ **T** 5. When an airline announces a plane will be delayed due to "mechanical problems," most people would have qualms about later boarding the plane.

_____ 6. When a person is really ill, a dependable doctor will give the person a placebo.

_____ **F** 7. Repeated trouble breathing could by a symptom of a dysfunction.

_____ 8. A man proposing to sell you his five-bedroom house on the beach in Malibu for $3,000 is probably making you a bona fide offer.

_____ **F** 9. Some malignant tumors can be removed.

_____ 10. When a person cannot name every country in the world, he or she should be worried about dementia.

2 Use the vocabulary words to complete the following analogies. For instructions on how to complete analogies, see the Analogies Appendix on page 159.

VOCABULARY LIST

paranoid	malignant	wary	perennial	dementia

SET ONE

1. a failing grade on a paper : disappointed :: a growling dog : _____

2. reading a good book : relaxing :: feeling that a killer lives on every block : _____

3. fleeting : _____ :: short : tall

4. cry : weep :: evil : _____

5. continually forgetting one's address : _____ :: laughter : happiness

VOCABULARY LIST

dysfunction	bona fide	placebo	qualm	inconsequential

SET TWO

6. dentist : drill :: hypochondriac : _____

7. a car seat : safe :: a diamond ring : _____

8. confidence : _____ :: cruelty : kindness

9. slipping on wet pavement : accident :: a bad kidney : _____

10. unimportant : _____ :: envy : jealousy

© 2005 Pearson Education, Inc.

3 Complete the following sentences using the vocabulary words. Use each word once.

VOCABULARY LIST

wary	dementia	dysfunction	placebo	bona fide
qualm	malignant	perennial	paranoid	inconsequential

1. My friend is _paranoid_ that someone is listening to his phone conversations, so sometimes we have to speak in code.

2. Even though they are _perennial_ losers, the town still supports the local baseball team because they are our team.

3. The historian wanted to make sure the manuscript was _bona fide_ before he began to use it for his paper on conditions during the Middle Ages.

4. My friend considered his comment about my bad cooking _inconsequential_, but I took it seriously. I was really trying to improve my cooking skills.

5. My colleague has misplaced his office keys six times this month, forgotten where he parked eight times, and missed three important meetings due to forgetfulness. I am getting worried that he may be suffering from _dementia_.

6. Four months after minor surgery my mother shouldn't be in pain, but she still wanted pills. At the family's request, the doctor began giving her a(n) _placebo_ a month ago. My mother insists she feels better after taking them.

7. My major _qualm_ about going camping this weekend is the weather. There is supposed to be a huge snowstorm in the mountains.

8. There was a(n) _dysfunction_ in the baby's heart, so the doctor had to do an operation soon after birth.

9. I am _wary_ of ads for products that claim to be able to make me look twenty years younger or make me rich in one month.

10. We were so happy that my friend's tumor was not _malignant_; she should be completely recovered in another year.

HINT

A World of Words

Keep your eyes open for new words. You will certainly encounter new words in the textbooks you read in college and in the lectures your professors give, but new words can be found everywhere. Don't turn off your learning when you leave the classroom. When you see a new word in a newspaper or a newsletter or even on a poster downtown, use the strategies you have learned in this book: look for context clues around the new word, try to predict the meaning, and check the dictionary if you aren't sure of the meaning. No matter where you are or at what age you may be, your vocabulary can continue to grow.

Complete the following lists.

Times people should be wary

1. _____

2. _____

Items one would want to make sure are bona fide

1. _____

2. _____

Signs of dementia

1. _____

2. _____

Actions of a paranoid

1. _____

2. _____

Problems that are inconsequential

1. _____

2. _____

Body parts that often become dysfunctional

1. _____

2. _____

Things that can be malignant

1. _____

2. _____

Perennial problems in society

1. _____

2. _____

Qualms freshmen have about college

1. _____

2. _____

Times when a placebo might be given

1. _____

2. _____

22 Linguistics

The World of Words

Language evolves. New words enter a language, and old words become **archaic**. "Ye Olde Barber Shoppe" would be an appropriate name for a hair salon in an historic district, but if you used "ye" in common speech for "the," people wouldn't understand you, or they'd find you a bit eccentric.

5   Some **neologisms** become part of a language, while others don't make it. In the last 150 years, people have tried to **coin** an **epicene**, or bisexual, pronoun. It can be awkward to always say "he or she" when speaking about a person of unknown gender. In the late 1800s Charles Crozat Converse coined a blended word formed from "that one." For ex-

10 ample, a sentence would read, "When a customer is angry, thon should be treated kindly." You wouldn't have to say, "He or she should be treated kindly." *Thon* was placed in a few dictionaries from 1898 to 1964 but never caught on with the speaking public. Today "they," "their," and "them" are being

15 used more and more as both singular and plural pronouns. These words have been used in the singular form for over one hundred years, but in some circles this use is still considered nonstandard and unacceptable.

    Neologisms are formed in many ways. New words can be

20 made by blending (such as *thon*), from people and place-names, and through abbreviations, among other methods. Blended words are also known as **portmanteau** words. Two common portmanteau words are *smog* from "smoke" and

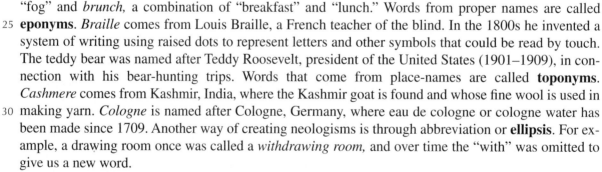

"fog" and *brunch,* a combination of "breakfast" and "lunch." Words from proper names are called

25 **eponyms**. *Braille* comes from Louis Braille, a French teacher of the blind. In the 1800s he invented a system of writing using raised dots to represent letters and other symbols that could be read by touch. The teddy bear was named after Teddy Roosevelt, president of the United States (1901–1909), in connection with his bear-hunting trips. Words that come from place-names are called **toponyms**. *Cashmere* comes from Kashmir, India, where the Kashmir goat is found and whose fine wool is used in

30 making yarn. *Cologne* is named after Cologne, Germany, where eau de cologne or cologne water has been made since 1709. Another way of creating neologisms is through abbreviation or **ellipsis**. For example, a drawing room once was called a *withdrawing room,* and over time the "with" was omitted to give us a new word.

    The field of **semantics** enriches our lives as we learn more about how languages are structured and

35 how they change. Learning the **etymology** of a word can help a person remember the meaning of the word, as well as being a fascinating way to see how language changes. The history of words shows that language is dynamic, and we can't expect or shouldn't even want a language to remain static. As the world changes so will the ways we talk about it. Everyone should enjoy having thon's chance to explore the wonder of words.

❚❚❚ PREDICTING

Cover the Word List below as you do the Predicting exercise. For each set, write the definition on the line next to the word to which it belongs. If you are unsure, return to the reading on page 112, and underline any context clues you find. After you've made your predictions, uncover the Word List and check your answers. Place a checkmark in the boxes next to the words whose definitions you missed. These are the words you'll want to study closely.

SET ONE

blending several features   to invent   new words   referring to either sex
a word rarely used today

❑   1. **archaic** (line 2) _____

❑   2. **neologisms** (line 5) _____

❑   3. **coin** (line 6) _____

❑   4. **epicene** (line 6) _____

❑   5. **portmanteau** (line 22) _____

SET TWO

the shortening of a word   words based on a person's name   the history of a word
names derived from the name of a place   a branch of linguistics that studies meaning

❑   6. **eponyms** (line 25) _____

❑   7. **toponyms** (line 28) _____

❑   8. **ellipsis** (line 31) _____

❑   9. **semantics** (line 34) _____

❑ 10. **etymology** (line 35) _____

❚❚❚ WORD LIST

archaic   *adj.*   1. of a word, often used in an
[är kā′ ik]   earlier time but rarely used today
               2. ancient, old-fashioned

coin   *v.*   1. to invent; to fabricate
[koin]   2. to make coins
      n.   a piece of metal money

ellipsis   *n.*   1. the shortening or abbreviation
[i lip′ sis]   of a word
           2. the omission from a sentence of
           a word or words that would make
           the sentence grammatically
           correct but aren't needed for
           clarity
           3. a mark, such as . . . , to indicate
           an omission of letters or words

epicene   *adj.*   1. of a noun or pronoun, capable
[ep′ i sēn′]   of referring to either sex
           2. characteristic of both sexes
           3. feeble, weak

eponym   *n.*   a word based on a person's name
[ep′ ə nim]

etymology   *n.*   the history of a word or part of
[et′ ə mol′ ə jē]   a word

neologism   *n.*   a new word or phrase or an
[nē ol′ ə jiz′ əm]   existing word used in a new way

portmanteau   *adj.*   combining or blending several
[pôrt man′ tō]   features or qualities
      n.   a case or bag to carry clothing in
          while traveling

semantics   *n.*   1. a branch of linguistics dealing
[si man′ tiks]   with the study of meaning,
          including the ways meaning
          changes over time
          2. the meaning or an
          interpretation of the meaning of
          a word, sign, or sentence.

toponym   *n.*   a word derived from the name
[top′ ə nim′]   of a place

1 Match each example with the correct vocabulary word.

VOCABULARY LIST

semantics	toponym	portmanteau	coin	archaic
eponym	etymology	ellipsis	epicene	neologism

1. Ferris wheel (G. W. G. Ferris) _____

2. motel ("motor" + "hotel") _____

3. cab (cabriolet) _____

4. hamburger (Hamburg)

   _____

5. thou _____

6. addict: Latin *addictus* assigned,
   surrendered _____

7. screen saver _____

8. himorher _____

9. "Let's call it a patuka."

   _____

10. "I think the line means that he is
    foolish to be 'wasting' his time." "I think the line means that he is relaxing by 'wasting' his time."

    _____

2 For each set, write the letter of the most logical analogy. See the Analogies Appendix on page 159 for instructions and practice.

SET ONE

_____ 1. sandwich : eponym ::	a. new inventions : neologisms
_____ 2. ancient : archaic ::	b. lengthening : ellipsis
_____ 3. rain : flowers grow ::	c. tennis : sport
_____ 4. hot : cold ::	d. look in a dictionary : etymology
_____ 5. phone rings : answer it ::	e. angry : mad

SET TWO

_____ 6. invent : coin ::	f. Bermuda shorts : toponym
_____ 7. round : flat ::	g. gardener : lawn mower
_____ 8. semantics : linguistics ::	h. strong : epicene
_____ 9. traveler : portmanteau ::	i. microbiology : biology
_____ 10. polka : a dance ::	j. couch : sofa

3 Complete each sentence using the vocabulary words. Use each word once.

VOCABULARY LIST

toponym	archaic	semantics	coin	portmanteau
ellipsis	neologism	epicene	eponym	etymology

1. Some of Juanita's habits are _____archaic_____, such as wearing white gloves when she goes out, but she is a sweet old lady.

2. I was suspicious of the ad because of the _____ellipsis_____ in it. I wondered what the original context was that had been shortened to "One reviewer calls it a '. . . great . . . ' show."

3. A(n) _____neologism_____ many people encounter every weekend is the food court.

4. I decided to check the _____etymology_____ of the word *anger* before I wrote a definition paper in English. My instructor said that looking up the history of a word was a good step in trying to explain what it means.

5. It was interesting to find out that *tangerine* is a(n) _____toponym_____ coming from Tangier, Morocco.

6. In science class we all had to invent something and then _____coined_____ a word for it.

7. It doesn't take much detective work to figure out that *platonic* is a(n) _____eponym_____ derived from the philosopher Plato.

8. The art exhibit was a(n) _____portmanteau_____ show with everything from paintings and sculptures to mobiles and pottery.

9. In my linguistics class, I found the area of _____semantics_____ especially interesting; I enjoyed seeing how the meanings of words have changed through time.

10. I thought it was a(n) _____epicene_____ excuse when Colin said he couldn't pick me up at the airport because his favorite team might be in the play-offs that night.

▌▐█▌ INTERACTIVE EXERCISE

Answer the following questions about the vocabulary words.

1. If your name became an eponym, what would it refer to?

_____

_____

2. Coin a word and give the definition of the word.

_____

_____

3. Name two fields that have created several neologisms in the last decade.

_____   _____

4. Come up with a toponym based on a place in your community. Explain why you picked this

place. _____

_____

5. What word do you think will become archaic in fifty years? Briefly explain your choice.

_____

_____

6. What would be your entry for an epicene pronoun?

_____

_____

7. Make up a portmanteau word and show what two words it comes from.

_____

_____

8. Look up the etymology of a word you find interesting and write the etymology here.

_____

_____

9. Use ellipsis to create a new word.

_____

_____

10. What word would it be easy to get into a semantic argument about?

_____

_____

23 Political Science

Searching for the Ideal

Political systems have come in many forms over the course of human history. The quest for a **utopian** form of government has run the **gamut** from monarchies to democracies. Ancient Rome and the Soviet Union are two examples separated by time and place that show the similarities and differences in how governments are run.

5   After the rule of a tyrannical king, the Romans formed a **republic** around 500 B.C. The senators of the republic worked together to make decisions regarding laws. This system worked well until Rome began to expand and it became harder to control the many lands Rome had conquered. Eventually military power became more important than laws. In 62 B.C. Julius Caesar proposed a **triumvirate** with himself, the general Pompey, and the rich banker Crassus. These three men ruled Rome through

10 bribery, fear, and other methods. When the triumvirate
collapsed, Pompey and
Caesar went to war. Caesar
won and became "Dictator

15 for Life"; there was even talk
of making Caesar a king.
Rome had gone from a re-
public to a **totalitarian** government. Caesar did make

20 improvements for the people
such as fixing the taxation
system, making living conditions easier in the conquered
territories, and changing the

Julius Caesar

Karl Marx

25 calendar. Still, his authoritar-
ian rule was not appreciated, and seeing no other way to **oust** him, a group of nobles murdered Caesar in the Senate on the Ides of March (March 15) in 44 B.C.

    In the 1800s the world was changing due to the rise of industrialism. The **milieu** was ripe for new ideas. Many people lived in slums and worked long hours in harsh conditions. Karl Marx was the

30 voice for this class. In 1867 he published *Das Kapital,* explaining the class struggle between the poor and the rich. The **proletariat** consisted of the workers who could gain power from the **bourgeoisie**, the property-owning capitalist class, only by revolution. Marx felt this revolution would take place in Germany or England where capitalism was well established, but it was Russia in 1917 that saw the start of communism. Lenin and Trotsky led the fight for workers' rights with Lenin becoming dictator

35 of the newly named Union of Soviet Socialist Republics (USSR). After Lenin's death in 1924, Stalin became dictator. Stalin began many reforms, but he also silenced all opposition. A totalitarian govern-ment was born again.

    The USSR was dissolved in 1991, and the ideological **underpinnings** of communism have been shaken. Capitalism continues to thrive worldwide, although workers still fight for fair wages and safe

40 working conditions. Humankind continues its search for an ideal form of government.

▐▐▌ PREDICTING

Cover the Word List below as you do the Predicting exercise. For each set, write the definition on the line next to the word to which it belongs. If you are unsure, return to the reading on page 117, and underline any context clues you find. After you've made your predictions, uncover the Word List and check your answers. Place a checkmark in the boxes next to the words whose definitions you missed. These are the words you'll want to study closely.

SET ONE

the entire range   resembling an ideal place   a government with three people in power
a government that uses dictatorial control   a state where power rests with the citizens

❑ 1. **utopian** (line 1) _____

❑ 2. **gamut** (line 2) _____

❑ 3. **republic** (line 5) _____

❑ 4. **triumvirate** (line 8) _____

❑ 5. **totalitarian** (line 18) _____

SET TWO

environment   a foundation   the working class   to remove
the property-owning class

❑ 6. **oust** (line 26) _____

❑ 7. **milieu** (line 28) _____

❑ 8. **proletariat** (line 31) _____

❑ 9. **bourgeoisie** (line 31) _____

❑ 10. **underpinnings** (line 38) _____

▐▐▌ WORD LIST

bourgeoisie
[boor′ zhwä zē′]
n. 1. in Marxist theory, the property-owning capitalist class
2. the middle class

gamut
[gam′ ət]
n. the entire scale or range

milieu
[mil yoo′]
n. environment; surroundings

oust
[oust]
v. to remove; to force out

proletariat
[prō′ li târ′ ē ət]
n. 1. in Marxist theory, the workers who do not own property and who must sell their labor to survive
2. the lowest or poorest class

republic
[ri pub′ lik]
n. 1. a state where power rests with the citizens
2. a state where the head of government is usually an elected president

totalitarian
[tō tal′ i târ′ ē ən]
adj. 1. pertaining to a government that uses dictatorial control and forbids opposition
2. authoritarian
n. an adherent of totalitarian principles or government

triumvirate
[trī um′ vər it, -və rāt′]
n. 1. a government of three rulers or officials functioning jointly
2. any group of three

underpinning
[un′ dər pin′ ing]
n. 1. a foundation or basis (often used in the plural)
2. material used to support a structure

utopian
[yoo tō′ pē ən]
adj. 1. resembling utopia, an ideal place
2. involving idealized perfection
3. given to impractical schemes of perfection

1 Circle the correct meaning of each vocabulary word.

1. utopian:	idealized	realized
2. republic:	power with a dictator	power with the people
3. bourgeoisie:	middle class	working class
4. triumvirate:	rule by one	rule by three
5. oust:	to remove	to add
6. gamut:	range	one and only
7. milieu:	emptiness	surroundings
8. proletariat:	working class	middle class
9. totalitarian:	liberal	authoritarian
10. underpinnings:	basis	conclusion

2 Answer each question by writing the vocabulary word on the line next to the example it best fits. Use each word once.

SET ONE

VOCABULARY LIST

oust	triumvirate	utopian	gamut	totalitarian

1. Reginald told his bike racing team that he would order all the team's clothing in the sizes he thought people needed, and he would decide which races people would go to. What kind of leader is he? _totalitarian_

2. The team decided to remove Reginald as their manager. What did they decide to do with him? _to oust_

3. Reginald cried and then laughed when the team told him he had to go. What can be said about his emotions? _gamut_

4. Reginald then joined with Karl and Miguel to be the leaders of a new team. What did the three of them form? _triumvirate_

5. The three men feel that they will never argue with each other and that their team will win every race. What is their outlook on life? _utopian_

VOCABULARY LIST

bourgeoisie	republic	proletariat	milieu	underpinnings

6. Keri just bought a house by the lake. What group has she become a part of according to Marxist theory? _bourgeoisie_

7. Matthew rents an apartment and works as a busboy. What group does he belong to following Marxist theory? _plotes,_

8. Keri and Matthew get to vote for the president of their country. What kind of political system does their country have? _rep_

9. Matthew and Keri became friends when they met in the park at a soccer game. An avid interest in sports has cemented their friendship. What is a term for the basis of a relationship? _underpinnings_

10. They both work in busy places: Keri in an office and Matthew at a restaurant. What is one's environment called? _milieu_   _milieu_

3 Complete the reading using each word once.

VOCABULARY LIST

underpinnings	milieu	triumvirate	utopian	bourgeoisie
proletariat	oust	republic	gamut	totalitarian

The Survey

For my political science class I took a survey asking students what life would be like in their (1) _utopian_ society. I was surprised at some of the responses I got. The answers ran the (2) _gamut_ from governments that gave citizens complete freedom to those that had strict control of a person's every move. I was surprised at first by the woman who favored a(n) (3) _t_ form of government, but the more I talked to her, the more I saw that she didn't like making any kind of decision. The (4) _underpinnings_ of most people's societies were freedom and equality. Most of the students favored a(n) (5) _rep_ and liked the idea of citizens getting to make decisions about laws. Most people didn't want a class society. Several students said they thought it was unfair how the (6) _bour_ had manipulated workers for years. A few people even felt that in an ideal society, everyone would belong to the (7) _prol._ and work together for the good of society, although several noted that this system hadn't been historically successful. Most people felt the (8) _milieu_ in the perfect society would be one of peace. One man wrote on his survey, "I'd (9) _oust_ any whiners from my town, and then life would be great." For fun, I asked my classmates what three people, dead or alive, they would pick if the government was run as a(n) (10) _triumvirate_. My favorite response was Oprah, Superman, and Princess Diana. The survey helped me write an excellent paper on people's views of society and government.

HINT

Banned Books

Freedom of expression has not always been a right granted to all people in all places. Over the centuries several books have been banned because of their content or wording. Many of the books that are now considered classics were banned at one time. A person doesn't have to like every book that is printed, but keeping an open mind about what one is asked to read in college or what one chooses to read later in life helps to foster creativity, critical thinking, and understanding in an individual.

The following are a few books that have been banned previously (Are any a surprise to you?):

Of Mice and Men by John Steinbeck
The Catcher in the Rye by J. D. Salinger
The House of Spirits by Isabel Allende
Beloved by Toni Morrison
Lord of the Flies by William Golding

The Color Purple by Alice Walker
James and the Giant Peach by Roald Dahl
To Kill a Mockingbird by Harper Lee
Bless Me Ultima by Rudolfo Anaya
Harry Potter (the series) by J. K. Rowling

▌█▌█ INTERACTIVE EXERCISE

Give two examples for each of the following situations.

EXAMPLE: milieu at a sporting event   _fans cheering_   _a scoreboard flashing_

1. **milieu** at a party   _____   _____
2. **proletariat** actions   _____   _____
3. **underpinnings** of a charity   _____   _____
4. characteristics of a **utopian** society   _____   _____
5. circumstances that would cause
   a company to **oust** its president   _____   _____
6. actions of a **totalitarian** government   _____   _____
7. a **gamut** of emotions   _____   _____
8. **bourgeoisie** behavior   _____   _____
9. actions in a **republic**   _____   _____
10. where a **triumvirate** could be found   _____   _____

24 Mathematics

More Than Numbers

To: Lucy
From: Kris
Date: Feb. 28, 2005
Re: Spring Display

Memo

5   It's time to design the spring window display. As you have a **finite** space to work with, you'll want to plan carefully. The company envisions a **symmetrical** design showing women's fashions on one side and men's on the other. We believe it is a **fallacy** of the fashion world that men's fashions aren't

10   important. We want both genders to be given equal space and attention in the display. We would like a **gradation** of pastel colors in the background going from a darker blue to a pale pink. We want a row of rabbits to **bisect** the display case, separating the men's and women's fashions. Using these

15   guidelines, we hope you can design a display that captures the energy of spring and the new, colorful fashion line.

MEMORANDUM

May 6, 2005

Alexander,

20   I've compiled some **statistics** and found that our production levels were below **quota** for the last quarter. The **interval** between New Year's Day and April 1 saw a 20% drop in output. Several **variables** could have caused the low numbers: the bad weather this winter, the flu that hit

25   40% of our workers, or that breakdown that took out 25% of our equipment for over a week. However, what I find to be the real **enigma** is why production jumped up 50% between March and

30   April. What are you doing over there? Send me a memo giving me your take on the situation.

Toni

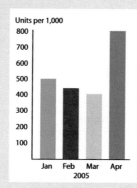

▮▮▮ PREDICTING

Cover the Word List below as you do the Predicting exercise. For each set, write the definition on the line next to the word to which it belongs. If you are unsure, return to the reading on page 122, and underline any context clues you find. After you've made your predictions, uncover the Word List and check your answers. Place a checkmark in the boxes next to the words whose definitions you missed. These are the words you'll want to study closely.

SET ONE

having limits   to divide into two equal parts   regular in arrangement of corresponding parts
the passing of one shade of color to another by small degrees   a misconception

❑ 1. **finite** (line 6) _____

❑ 2. **symmetrical** (line 7) _____

❑ 3. **fallacy** (line 9) _____

❑ 4. **gradation** (line 11) _____

❑ 5. **bisect** (line 13) _____

SET TWO

a part of a total amount   a time between events   a puzzling occurrence
numerical facts   things that change

❑ 6. **statistics** (line 20) _____

❑ 7. **quota** (line 21) _____

❑ 8. **interval** (line 21) _____

❑ 9. **variables** (line 23) _____

❑ 10. **enigma** (line 28) _____

▮▮▮ WORD LIST

bisect
[bī sekt′, bī′ sekt]
v. 1. to cut or divide into two equal or approximately equal parts
2. to intersect or cross

enigma
[ə nig′ mə]
n. 1. a puzzling occurrence or person
2. a riddle

fallacy
[fal′ ə sē]
n. 1. a misconception; a misleading belief
2. an unsound argument

finite
[fī′ nīt]
adj. having bounds or limits; measurable

gradation
[grā dā′ shən]
n. 1. the passing of one tint or shade of color to another by small degrees
2. change taking place through stages or gradually
3. a stage in a series

interval
[in′ tər vəl]
n. 1. a time between events; a pause
2. a space between things

quota
[kwō′ tə]
n. 1. a part of a total amount; an allotment
2. the number or percentage of people of a specified kind allowed into a group or institution

statistics
[stə tis′ tiks]
n. 1. (used with a plural v.) data; numerical facts
2. (used with a singular v.) the science that deals with the collection and study of numerical data

symmetrical
[si me′ tri kəl]
adj. regular in form or arrangement of corresponding parts

variable
[vâr′ ē ə bəl]
n. something that may or does change
adj. 1. changeable; inconstant
2. having diversity

1 Put a T for true or F for false next to each sentence.

_____ 1. Statistics can be manipulated.

___T__ 2. A house has a finite amount of space.

___T__ 3. The exact circumstances of John F. Kennedy's death are an enigma.

_____ 4. Having a small triangle on one side of a picture and five large circles on the other side would be a symmetrical arrangement.

_____ 5. The weather in the United States is rarely variable.

_____ 6. It is a fallacy that studying helps students learn.

_____ 7. A thirty-degree change in temperature in ten minutes is an example of gradation.

___T__ 8. The interval between a job interview and being accepted or rejected can make a person nervous.

___F__ 9. It could be difficult to fill one's quota of strawberries to be picked if the person stops to eat several every five minutes.

_____ 10. If you cut a cake in nine pieces, you have bisected it.

2 In each group, circle the word that does not have a connection to the other three words. See Chapter 3 for an example.

1. clear	enigma	riddle	puzzle
2. finite	measurable	limited	infinite
3. stage	degree	fixed	gradation
4. data	statistics	figures	words
5. diverse	steady	changeable	variable
6. divide	join	bisect	intersect
7. fallacy	misleading	truth	misconception
8. whole	part	quota	allotment
9. balanced	regular	asymmetrical	symmetrical
10. pause	space	interval	continuous

3 Complete the following analogies. See the Analogies Appendix on page 159 for instructions on how to complete analogies.

VOCABULARY LIST

enigma	finite	interval	statistics	variable
bisect	fallacy	gradation	quota	symmetrical

1. long : short :: infinite : _____

2. skyscrapers : tall :: interest rates : _____

3. old : elderly :: misconception : _____

4. boring : exciting :: unbalanced : _____

5. what is at the far reaches of the universe : _____ :: poodle : dog

6. portion : _____ :: silence : hush

7. hem : a skirt :: _____ : a circle

8. a half hour : _____ :: fog : weather

9. bright : shiny :: stages : _____

10. government : _____ :: cook : stove

▌▐ ▌▐ ▌ INTERACTIVE EXERCISE

Following the example of the reading on page 122, pick another field that could use mathematical terms, and write a memo using six of the vocabulary words. Occupations that you might consider are construction, coaching, banking, and interior design.

Memo

To: _____

From: _____

Date: _____

Re: _____

_____

_____

_____

_____

_____

_____

_____

_____

25 Word Parts III

Look for words with these **prefixes**, **roots**, and/or **suffixes** as you work through this book. You may have already seen some of them, and you will see others in later chapters. Learning basic word parts can help you figure out the meanings of unfamiliar words.

prefix: a word part added to the beginning of a word that changes the meaning of the root
root: a word's basic part with its essential meaning
suffix: a word part added to the end of a word; indicates the part of speech

WORD PART	MEANING	EXAMPLES AND DEFINITIONS
Prefixes		
ad-	to, toward, near	*adhere:* to hold closely or firmly *adjacent:* lying near or close
dys-	faulty, bad, ill	*dysfunctional:* faulty operation *dyslexia:* any of various reading disorders
meta-	change	*metamorphosis:* a change in form *metabolism:* the physical and chemical changes in an organism that make energy available
neo-	new, revived, modified	*neologism:* a new word or phrase *neoclassical:* pertaining to a revival of classical styles in art, literature, music, or architecture
para-	next to, almost, beyond, abnormal	*paraphrase:* a restatement of a passage *parallel:* going in the same direction; next to each other
Roots		
-annu-, -enni-	year	*biannual:* happening twice each year *perennial:* lasting throughout the entire year
-esce-	becoming	*acquiesce:* to become agreeable *convalesce:* to become well after an illness
-fid-	faith, trust	*bona fide:* done in good faith *confide:* to have trust
-grad-, -gress	to step	*retrograde:* to step backward; to retire or retreat *transgress:* to step across a limit; to violate
-mut-	change	*permutation:* the act of changing *mutant:* a new type of organism due to a change in a gene or chromosome

WORD PART	MEANING	EXAMPLES AND DEFINITIONS
-sequ-	to follow	*inconsequential:* not following in thought; illogical *sequel:* a literary work or film that follows the same story of a preceding work
-tract-	to drag, to pull, to draw	*intractable:* stubborn; hard to pull *tractor:* a vehicle used to pull things
Suffixes		
-esque (makes an adjective)	resembling, relating to	*picturesque:* resembling a picture *Romanesque:* relating to Rome
-oid (makes an adjective)	like, resembling	*paranoid:* like or suffering from paranoia (an excessive distrust of others) *humanoid:* resembling humans
-ure (makes a verb)	action or process	*censure:* process of expressing disapproval *failure:* action of failing

▌▌▌ SELF-TESTS

1 Read each definition and choose the appropriate word. Use each word once. The meaning of the word part is underlined to help you make the connection. Refer to the Word Parts list if you need help.

VOCABULARY LIST

adjoin	gradual	asteroid	commute	inure
sequence	obsolescent	neonate	confidant	paraprofessional

1. star<u>like</u>   *asteroid*
2. the <u>process</u> of coming into use   *inure*
3. to be <u>near</u> or in contact with   *adjoin*
4. a <u>newborn</u> child   *neonate*
5. a person trained to work <u>next to</u> a doctor, lawyer, teacher, or other professional   *paraprofessional*
6. <u>becoming</u> useless   *obsolescent*
7. a person one puts <u>trust</u> in   *confidant*
8. changing by small degrees or <u>step-by-step</u>   *gradual*
9. to <u>change</u> a penalty to a less severe form   *commute*
10. the <u>following</u> of one thing after another   *sequence*

2 Finish the sentences with the meaning of each word part. Use each meaning once. The word part is underlined to help you make the connection.

VOCABULARY LIST

draw	becoming	revived	process	bad
year	resemble	step	toward	faith

1. Androids are popular characters in science fiction movies because they ___resemble___ human beings; therefore, they are easy to costume.

2. I admired the painting so much that I bought it. Maybe it was the red hues, but something kept drawing me ___toward___ it.

3. The book I just finished is a good example of neoromanticism. It ___revived___ the romantic movement's interest in the importance of nature.

4. My nephew's adolescence is almost over; he will be seventeen next month, and I can see how he is ___becoming___ an adult.

5. When I graduate from college, I will be one ___step___ closer to being an independent woman.

6. I was able to procure the special chocolates my husband likes, but the ___process___ wasn't easy. I called five places before I was given an address where I could order them, and then it took eight weeks for the box to arrive.

7. I am not worried about my girlfriend's fidelity; I have ___faith___ in her loyalty.

8. My husband forgot our anniversary, which shouldn't surprise me. He forgets it every ___year___.

9. The store was able to ___draw___ me in with their attractive window display.

10. I have been suffering from dysphoria ever since the weather turned ugly. Among the ___bad___ feelings I am experiencing are restlessness and anxiety.

3 Finish the story using the word parts. Use each word part once. Your knowledge of word parts, as well as the context clues, will help you create the correct words. If you do not understand the meaning of a word you have made, check the dictionary for the definition or to see whether the word exists.

WORD PARTS

esque	ad	neo	gress	annu
meta	fid	mut	tract	ure

The Run

It was time for the town's ___annu___al Mud Run, and this year I was going to participate for the first time. Being a ___neo___phyte, I wasn't sure what to expect. I hoped I could end___ure___ the distance, the hills, and, most of all, the mud on the course. I was a bit intimidated when I saw my statu___esque___ competitors at the starting line. They all looked like they had stepped off a pedestal at a Greek temple. Then I started

to hear the animal _meta_phors: "I'm a stampeding elephant," "I'm a leopard waiting to leap." I became an ostrich ready to put my head in the sand. But I got my con_fid_ence back and took off with everyone else when the gun sounded. My pro_gress_ was hindered at the first water crossing. I was afraid to get too wet, but I didn't want to pro_tract_ the race, so I jumped in and got soaked. We did three laps, and every lap there was some _tract_ation in the course. With all the runners going by, the conditions changed each lap. The dirt just kept getting worse. Finally, I crossed the finish line in third place. I was overjoyed. I also became an _ad_dict for mud runs. I have since competed in over one hundred races.

4 Pick the best definition for each underlined word using your knowledge of word parts. Circle the word part in each of the underlined words.

a. relating to the writings of Franz Kafka

b. resembling the truth but unproven

c. to become one; to unite

d. unchangeable

e. a person who changes a literary work from one form to another

f. beyond the usual

g. a comment that doesn't follow the preceding one

h. to draw away; to take a part

i. happening every two years

j. an inability to speak or understand words because of an illness in the brain

_____ 1. The Internet has helped to spread several <u>factoids</u>; people read the same stories about killer bananas or ways to earn thousands of dollars and think the stories are real.

_____ 2. Curtis is studying <u>paranormal</u> activities such as <u>clairvoyance</u> and extrasensory perception.

_____ 3. My cousin is suffering from <u>dysphasia</u>. It is difficult to communicate with her.

_____ 4. My life at work has become <u>Kafkaesque</u> since the new manager insists on changing procedures without telling anyone. I am never sure what is going on anymore.

_____ 5. The ideas for my research paper finally <u>coalesced</u> after a good night's sleep.

_____ 6. Unfortunately, Verda was <u>immutable</u> about her vacation plans, and she went to the mountains to ski even though there wasn't any snow.

_____ 7. I found it hard to understand the speaker because his speech was filled with <u>non sequiturs</u>. His comments just didn't connect to one another.

_____ 8. The Olympics are a <u>biennial</u> celebration of athletics worldwide.

_____ 9. The pile of boxes in the driveway <u>detracted</u> from the overall appeal of the house.

_____ 10. My uncle is a <u>metaphrast</u>; he changes short stories into poems.

5 A good way to remember word parts is to pick one word that uses a word part and understand how that word part functions in the word. Then you can apply that meaning to other words that have the same word part. Use the words to help you match the word part to its meaning.

SET ONE

_____ 1. **ad-:** adhere, adore, adjoin   a. to follow

_____ 2. **-esce-:** acquiesce, adolescent, luminescent   b. becoming

_____ 3. **-fid-:** confide, fidelity, bona fide   c. to, toward, near

_____ 4. **-sequ-:** sequence, sequel, consequence   d. faith, trust

_____ 5. **-oid:** humanoid, paranoid, android   e. resembling, like

SET TWO

_____ 6. **para-:** parallel, parasite, paranormal   f. to step

_____ 7. **-grad-, -gress-:** progress, gradual, transgress   g. year

_____ 8. **-mut-:** permutation, commute, mutation   h. action or process

_____ 9. **-annu-, -enni-:** annual, anniversary, perennial   i. change

_____ 10. **-ure:** censure, endure, procedure   j. next to, almost, beyond, abnormal

---

HINT

Play with Words

To make reading and vocabulary fun, learn to enjoy using words in recreational settings.
- Pick up the newspaper and do the crossword puzzle.
- Buy popular board games that are based on using words such as Scrabble, Boggle, or Scattergories. Invite your friends over to play.
- Play word games when traveling—for example, the first person says a type of food and the next person must say a word that begins with the last letter of the previous word: pizza, apple, eggplant, tomato, oatmeal. Pick another category when no one can think of a new word to fit the last letter.
- Write cards, letters, or e-mail messages that play with language—for example, write a thank-you note that uses several synonyms to express how "kind" your friend was: tender, considerate, amiable, compassionate, solicitous, obliging, benevolent, sensitive. Your friends will enjoy getting your letters and e-mails, and they will appreciate learning new words too.

6 Use the dictionary to find a word you don't know that uses the word part. Write the meaning of the word part, the word, and the definition. If your dictionary has the etymology (history) of the word, see how the word part relates to the meaning, and write the etymology after the definition.

Word Part	Meaning	Word	Definition and Etymology
EXAMPLE:			
-sequ-	to follow	sequela	an abnormal condition resulting from a previous disease. From Latin sequela, what follows
1. *annu-*			
2. *meta-*			
3. *mut-*			
4. *neo-*			
5. *tract-*			

26 Anthropology

Societies and Customs

The Mayan culture continues to intrigue modern society. One of the great centers of Mayan culture was Chichén Itzá on the Yucatán Peninsula. Life at Chichén Itzá was hardly **immutable**. Roughly between the years 500 and 1400, numerous temples, a huge ball court, and an astronomical observatory **burgeoned** in the tropical jungle. The Maya

5 abandoned the site twice, and around 1200 the Toltecs from the north invaded the area, adding their religion and architecture to the Mayan concepts. Anthropologists and archeologists have been **meticulous** in studying the ruins at

10 Chichén Itzá to discover the customs of this ancient society.

What made life **viable** for the Maya at Chichén Itzá were the *cenotes,* or wells. These wells provided a source of water for a commu-

15 nity of slaves, merchants, warriors, farmers, hunters, priests, and nobles. The cenotes also hold a clue to the religious customs of the Maya: several bodies have been found in the wells. Human sacrifice, although generally con-

20 sidered **heinous** by today's standards, was a part of Mayan religious practices. The Maya had several gods, and the sacrifices may have been used to **quell** the **wrath** of a rain god or pay homage to the god of maize. Bloodletting, especially of the

25 ears and tongue, was another way a person could **garner** favor with a god.

The Castillo

A chacmool figure introduced by the Toltecs, possibly used in heart sacrifices.

Religious beliefs were also **manifested** in the architecture and games of the Maya. An impressive and **ominous** area at Chichén Itzá is the Great Ball Court, the largest found at a Mayan site. The

30 ball game was played between two teams and seems to have involved keeping a rubber ball from touching the ground without using the hands. The game was over when the ball went through a scoring ring attached to the walls of the court, and the winner of the game did not receive the prize people today would expect: the captain of the winning team would

35 offer his head to the leader of the losing team for decapitation. It was part of the Mayan religious beliefs that dying quickly was a great honor, and they obviously felt that the winner of this contest deserved such an honor.

The Maya were a highly advanced society, demonstrated in their complex temple designs, accurate calendar, and elaborate artwork. The Maya continue to fascinate the world with their customs and

40 achievements.

▌▮▌ PREDICTING

Cover the Word List below as you do the Predicting exercise. For each set, write the definition on the line next to the word to which it belongs. If you are unsure, return to the reading on page 132, and underline any context clues you find. After you've made your predictions, uncover the Word List and check your answers. Place a checkmark in the boxes next to the words whose definitions you missed. These are the words you'll want to study closely.

SET ONE

possible	flourished	unchangeable	evil	extremely	careful

- ❏ 1. **immutable** (line 2) _____
- ❏ 2. **burgeoned** (line 4) _____
- ❏ 3. **meticulous** (line 9) _____
- ❏ 4. **viable** (line 12) _____
- ❏ 5. **heinous** (line 20) _____

SET TWO

rage	revealed	to get	to quiet	threatening

- ❏ 6. **quell** (line 23) _____
- ❏ 7. **wrath** (line 23) _____
- ❏ 8. **garner** (line 25) _____
- ❏ 9. **manifested** (line 27) _____
- ❏ 10. **ominous** (line 28) _____

▌▮▌ WORD LIST

burgeon
[bûr′ jən]
v. to flourish; to grow; to sprout

garner
[gär′ nər]
v. to acquire; to collect; to get

heinous
[hā′ nəs]
adj. wicked; vile; evil

immutable
[i myoo′ tə bəl]
adj. unchangeable

manifest
[man′ ə fest′]
v. to reveal; to show plainly
adj. obvious; evident
n. a list of cargo or passengers

meticulous
[mə tik′ yə ləs]
adj. 1. extremely careful and precise
2. excessively concerned with details

ominous
[om′ ə nəs]
adj. 1. foreboding; threatening; menacing
2. pertaining to an evil omen

quell
[kwel]
v. 1. to quiet; to pacify
2. to suppress

viable
[vī′ ə bəl]
adj. 1. practicable; possible
2. capable of living or developing

wrath
[rath, räth]
n. rage; fury; violent anger

1 Match each term with its synonym in Set One and its antonym in Set Two.

SYNONYMS

SET ONE

_____	1. heinous	a. workable
_____	2. quell	b. blossom
_____	3. meticulous	c. calm
_____	4. burgeon	d. vicious
_____	5. viable	e. thorough

ANTONYMS

SET TWO

_____	6. garner	f. patience
_____	7. immutable	g. hidden
_____	8. wrath	h. lose
_____	9. ominous	i. changeable
_____	10. manifest	j. safe

2 Complete the sentences using the vocabulary words. Use each word once.

VOCABULARY LIST

garner	immutable	meticulous	quell	wrath
burgeoned	heinous	manifest	viable	ominous

1. My mother's negative reaction was ___burgeoned___ _(immutable)_ about my little sister taking a trip to India with a man she met a month ago.

2. I need to ___garner___ more evidence about the people of the Andes to write my paper.

3. Alicia was quick to ___quell___ the rumor that she was engaged to Brian; she assured people they were just friends.

4. The ___heinous___ music signaled the entrance of the villain.

5. The people decided that the mountain was not a(n) ___viable___ place to live after their crops failed two years in a row.

6. His love for Amanda was ___manifest___ to everyone but Carlos.

7. It was a(n) ___ominous___ action by the vandals to break all the windows in the auditorium the day before the graduation ceremony.

8. I was ___meticulous___ in following the instructions for the cake, so I don't understand why it tasted horrible.

9. Wanda's confidence ___burgeoned___ when she got an A on her first paper.

10. The players felt their coaches' ___wrath___ at halftime. The team was twenty points behind and had made some stupid mistakes.

3 Complete the readings using each word once.

DAY 1

VOCABULARY LIST

garner	burgeoned	meticulous	viable	immutable

The plane is about to take off. I am so excited about my summer trip to the South Pacific to (1) _garner_ information on how the local people live. I remember how my interest in anthropology (2) _burgeoned_ after I read Margaret Mead's book *The Coming of Age in Samoa.* Her (3) _meticulous_ work in observing and recording the behaviors of the people fascinated me. I wasn't sure that making a living as an anthropologist was a(n) (4) _viable_ idea, but when I started college two years ago, I decided to pursue a subject I love. I know that the society I am about to visit has not been (5) _immutable_, but I hope to see some of the practices that my hero Mead saw.

DAY 5

VOCABULARY LIST

heinous	ominous	wrath	quell	manifest

Today we visited an army of ancient stone figures used to guard a sacred ceremonial site. The faces were (6) _heinous_ with big red eyes and long tongues sticking out of huge mouths. If someone dared to walk past the statues, he or she was sure to incur the (7) _wrath_ of the gods. The natives believed that (8) _ominous_ problems would befall a person who entered the taboo area. Because of the strong belief in a statue's power, diseases could (9) _manifest_ themselves in a person. It took herbal medicines and potent ceremonies to (10) _quell_ the fears and difficulties of those that disturbed the sacred place.

Pretend you have the opportunity to interview an anthropologist. Write six questions you would ask the person using at least six of the vocabulary words. You don't need to know the answers to the questions. Pick one or more societies to ask about. For example: How would you garner information about the burial practices of the Egyptians?

1. _____

   _____

2. _____

   _____

3. _____

   _____

4. _____

   _____

5. _____

   _____

6. _____

   _____

27 Geology

Our Earth

Letters

Lots to Learn

I didn't know much about the **lapidary** process until I read your article on gems ("Wonders of
5 the Earth," March/April issue). It was fascinating to learn that diamonds are the hardest substance known to humans and that their **impervious** nature also makes them important for industrial uses such as grinding. The history
10 of stonecutting, especially how **facets** are used, was engaging, and the illustrations were impressive. I continue to **oscillate** between the brilliant and rose-cut as my favorite—maybe I'll end up getting a diamond done each way!

15   **Thomas Ramzee**
                                        Selma, CA

Mysterious Powers

Your history of the magical powers **attributed** to gems was marvelous. I was amazed that the
20 use of gems as **amulets** goes back to the Egyptians. The various beliefs in gems as charms were astounding. I found especially intriguing the idea that placing an emerald under the tongue could allow a person to make
25 prophecies. **Vestiges** of the old beliefs obviously remain as people still associate rubies with love and happiness. I may even get a turquoise necklace to protect myself against accidents when I go horseback riding this summer. Thanks
30 for the tips.

                                    Clara Martinez
                                      Courterville, NC

"I am thankful that I have a diamond ring to protect me against ghosts!"   35

Judging Gems

I always thought it was the **luster** of gems that attracted people to them. Now I understand that besides brightness, other important qualities in judging gemstones are color, rarity, and hard- 40 ness. Your article also helped me learn that it isn't only the **inherent** qualities that lure people to a certain gem. I am thankful that I have a diamond ring to protect me against ghosts! It was a **magnanimous** gesture on the part of Lord Potter 45 to allow his collection to be photographed for the article. The pictures were gorgeous.

                                    Nettie Carlette
                                      Las Flores, NM

Our Earth welcomes readers' letters.   50
Please send them to Letters, 1158 Eighth Street, Centerton, NH, 03301, or e-mail us:
letters@ourearth.com.

▗▖▌▌ PREDICTING

Cover the Word List below as you do the Predicting exercise. For each set, write the definition on the line next to the word to which it belongs. If you are unsure, return to the reading on page 137, and underline any context clues you find. After you've made your predictions, uncover the Word List and check your answers. Place a checkmark in the boxes next to the words whose definitions you missed. These are the words you'll want to study closely.

SET ONE

to waver   incapable of being injured   considered as a quality of the thing indicated
the small polished plane surfaces of a cut gem   pertaining to the cutting of precious stones

☐ 1. **lapidary** (line 3) _____

☐ 2. **impervious** (line 8) _____

☐ 3. **facets** (line 10) _____

☐ 4. **oscillate** (line 12) _____

☐ 5. **attributed** (line 18) _____

SET TWO

brightness   unselfish   charms   traces of something   innate

☐ 6. **amulets** (line 20) _____

☐ 7. **vestiges** (line 25) _____

☐ 8. **luster** (line 37) _____

☐ 9. **inherent** (line 42) _____

☐ 10. **magnanimous** (line 45) _____

▌▐▌ WORD LIST

amulet
[am′ yə lit]
n. a charm worn to ward off evil or to bring good luck

attribute
[v. ə trib′ yo͞ot]
[n. a′ trə byo͞ot′]
v. 1. to consider as a quality of the person or thing indicated
2. to regard as resulting from a specified cause
n. 1. a quality or characteristic belonging to a person or thing
2. an object associated with a character or quality

facet
[fas′ it]
n. 1. one of the small polished plane surfaces of a cut gem
2. an aspect or phase

impervious
[im pûr′ vē əs]
adj. 1. incapable of being injured, impaired, or influenced
2. not permitting passage

inherent
[in hēr′ ənt, -her′]
adj. existing in someone or something as a permanent quality; innate

lapidary
[lap′ i der′ ē]
adj. pertaining to the cutting or engraving of precious stones
n. a worker who cuts, polishes, and engraves precious stones

luster
[lus′ tər]
n. 1. brightness; brilliance
2. distinction or glory

magnanimous
[mag nan′ ə məs]
adj. showing a noble spirit; generous in forgiving; unselfish

oscillate
[os′ ə lāt′]
v. 1. to waver between different beliefs or ideas
2. to swing or move back and forth

vestige
[ves′ tij]
n. 1. a trace of something that is no longer in existence
2. a slight amount of something

SELF-TESTS

1 Put a T for true or F for false next to each statement.

_____ 1. Using a shield made of paper would make a person impervious.

_____ 2. Studying should be a facet of every student's life.

_____ 3. Wearing an amulet is likely to help a student do well on a test even if he or she has not studied at all.

_____ 4. The Coliseum and Forum in Rome are vestiges of the once great Roman Empire.

_____ 5. Offering to give a fellow student a ride home after his car breaks down even though it is fifteen miles out of your way would be a magnanimous gesture.

_____ 6. You should go to a lapidary to get a clasp fixed on a necklace.

_____ 7. The need for sleep is inherent for all people.

_____ 8. It would be wise to attribute one's success on a test to the shoes one wore that day.

_____ 9. The luster of a great athlete's career can be damaged if the person is found guilty of using drugs to enhance performance.

_____ 10. It is not unusual for a student to oscillate when choosing a major.

2 Match the quotation to the word it best illustrates. Use each word once.

VOCABULARY LIST

attribute	impervious	lapidary	magnanimous	vestige
amulet	facet	inherent	luster	oscillate

1. "I tried to convince my father to let me go to the concert, but he wouldn't let me."
   _____impervious_____

2. "I have a little hope left, but not much." _____

3. "I'm unsure whether to major in English or history." _____

4. "I'm wearing this to protect me from evil spirits." _____

5. "The poor design of the intersection caused the accident." _____

6. "That was kind of Athena to forgive me for breaking her lamp." _____

7. "Kindness is part of her nature." _____

8. "The brilliance of her writing moved me." _____

9. "Every phase of the plan was double-checked to make sure it would run smoothly."

   _____

10. "I appreciate the way this emerald was shaped." _____

3 Circle the word that correctly completes each sentence.

1. Kathy wears a sapphire (vestige, amulet) when she goes hiking to protect her from snake bites.

2. Lewis stole the (facet, luster) of my announcement about becoming a supervisor by announcing that he was just promoted to vice president at his company.

3. Tragedy is as (magnanimous, inherent) to life as comedy.

4. Roberto's finest (luster, attribute) is the way he can make people laugh.

5. Luckily our tent was (inherent, impervious) to water because it rained all night.

6. A charred potbelly stove was the only (amulet, vestige) of our winter cabin.

7. Every (luster, facet) in the diamond contributes to its brilliance.

8. Thanks to Connie's (magnanimous, impervious) gesture of letting us use her house, we were able to hold our fund-raiser.

9. I took my ruby to the (vestige, lapidary) to have it cut after I noticed a flaw in it.

10. My hammock (attributed, oscillated) wildly as my nephew tried to wake me.

HINT

Reading for Pleasure

It might sound obvious, but many people forget that reading for fun makes a better reader overall. If you think you don't like to read, search for reading material about a subject that interests you. Textbooks are not always the most exciting reading material, so don't give up if you don't enjoy what you are currently required to read.

Assess your reading interests:

- Do you like to keep up on current events? Become a newspaper or weekly news-magazine reader.
- Do you have a hobby? Subscribe to a magazine on the topic.
- Do you like to look into people's lives? Pick up a collection of short stories or a novel. You can find everything from romance to mystery in fiction writing.
- Is there a time period you are interested in? Nonfiction and fiction books deal with events from ancient Egypt to the unknown future.
- Are you interested in travel or different countries? Try books by authors from foreign lands.

Become involved with what you read. Ask yourself questions about the reading, make connections to your life, and put yourself in a story by imagining yourself in a character's situation. What would you do if you had to stop an alien invasion, cope with a broken heart, or solve a murder? Look for the author's message as you read. Ask yourself what point the author is trying to get across. Do you agree or disagree with the author's point? By making connections to a reading, you will want to keep reading to see what happens.

Visit the library to try out different types of reading material. It's free! Also explore the Internet for various reading sources. Finding the type of reading material that is right for your personality and interests and becoming involved with the author's ideas will make reading fun, will lead to better reading skills, and will even make mandatory reading more productive.

INTERACTIVE EXERCISE

Write a letter to *Our Earth* using at least six of the vocabulary words.

_____

_____

_____

_____

_____

_____

_____

_____

_____

_____

_____

_____

_____

_____

_____

_____

_____

_____

_____

_____

_____

_____

_____

_____

_____

_____

_____

_____

_____

_____

CHAPTER 28 Education

Ways of Learning

There is no one right way to teach, just as there is no one right way to learn. What works for one student doesn't necessarily work for another. **Pedagogy** has undergone many **permutations** in the search for the best way to educate the most people. In 1983 psychologist Howard Gardner proposed a theory of seven types of intelligence. The Multiple Intelligences (MI) concept posits the idea that people learn dif-
5 ferently. Certainly knowing one's own preferred learning style should help that person learn better.

Two of Gardner's intelligences that most people are familiar with are the linguistic and logical-mathematical. The linguistic learner is the person who enjoys writing and reading, while the logical-mathematical learner enjoys arithmetic problems, strategy games, and experiments. **Kinesthetic** learners may have some trouble sitting at a desk all day because they learn best through movement.
10 Students who learn best this way can be good athletes and dancers. They also prefer **tactile** projects such as woodworking or cooking; these learners benefit most from hands-on
15 activities. Spatial learners **assimilate** information through pictures or images. They **relish** spending time with mazes, jigsaw puzzles, or drawings. Musical students delight in singing
20 or playing instruments. They are especially attentive to the sounds around them. Interpersonal learners like to work with others; they are good at communicating and understanding how other people feel. Lastly, intrapersonal learners look within themselves and are sensitive
25 to their own feelings.

By being knowledgeable about different learning styles, educators are able to use an **interdisciplinary** approach to teaching. To bring in the linguistic learner, a math instructor has her students read about famous mathematicians and asks students to write about their math problems. An English professor created a project where students connect a reading to a song to aid the
30 musical learner. There are several ways to make an assignment **germane** to the various learning styles. Another concern of educators is that evaluating learning has many **subjective** elements to it. For instance, it can be hard to point out exactly why a student's art project should get a B or a C. Art is usually judged by personal tastes, and what appeals to one person may repel another person. By using the concept of Multiple Intelligences, educators give students the chance to learn via their strengths and to
35 show what they have learned in a way that is meaningful to them. As education theories **coalesce**, society has come to discover that uniting ideas can bring out the best in everyone.

Cover the Word List below as you do the Predicting exercise. For each set, write the definition on the line next to the word to which it belongs. If you are unsure, return to the reading on page 142, and underline any context clues you find. After you've made your predictions, uncover the Word List and check your answers. Place a checkmark in the boxes next to the words whose definitions you missed. These are the words you'll want to study closely.

SET ONE

pertaining to touch   alterations   education   to absorb   relating to movement

☐   1.   **pedagogy** (line 2) _____

☐   2.   **permutations** (line 2) _____

☐   3.   **kinesthetic** (line 8) _____

☐   4.   **tactile** (line 12) _____

☐   5.   **assimilate** (line 15) _____

SET TWO

relevant   to unite   to enjoy   personal   involving two or more fields

☐   6.   **relish** (line 17) _____

☐   7.   **interdisciplinary** (line 27) _____

☐   8.   **germane** (line 30) _____

☐   9.   **subjective** (line 31) _____

☐   10.   **coalesce** (line 35) _____

▮▮▮ WORD LIST

assimilate
[ə sim′ ə lāt′]
v. 1. to absorb and incorporate
2. to make similar

coalesce
[kō′ ə les′]
v. to unite; to join together

germane
[jər mān′]
adj. closely related; relevant; pertinent

interdisciplinary
[in′ tər dis′ ə plə ner′ ē]
adj. involving two or more disciplines or fields

kinesthetic
[kin′ əs thet′ ik]
adj. relating to kinesthesia, the ability to feel movement of the limbs and body

pedagogy
[ped′ ə gō′ jē, -goj′ ē]
n. the art or science of teaching; education; instructional methods

permutation
[pûr′ myoo tā′ shən]
n. alteration; transformation

relish
[rel′ ish]
v. 1. to enjoy; to take pleasure in
2. to like the taste of
n. pleasurable appreciation of anything; liking

subjective
[səb jek′ tiv]
adj. 1. particular to an individual; personal
2. biased; nonobjective
3. taking place in the mind

tactile
[tak′ til, -tīl]
adj. 1. pertaining to the sense of touch
2. perceptible to the sense of touch; tangible

1 For each set, write the letter of the most logical analogy. See the Analogies Appendix on page 159 for instructions and practice.

SET ONE

_____ 1. faulty : flawed ::   a. instructor : pedagogy

_____ 2. impossible : likely ::   b. separate : coalesce

_____ 3. photographer : camera ::   c. dessert : relish

_____ 4. losing : disappointment :: d. variation : permutation

_____ 5. comedy : laugh ::   e. jumping : kinesthetic

SET TWO

_____ 6. sunset : visual ::   f. read : assimilate

_____ 7. farewell : good-bye ::   g. objective : subjective

_____ 8. cow : animal ::   h. relevant : germane

_____ 9. yell : whisper ::   i. a shower : tactile

_____ 10. pour : drink ::   j. sociolinguistics : interdisciplinary

2 Finish the following fictitious headlines. Use each word once.

VOCABULARY LIST

permutation	subjective	germane	assimilate	interdisciplinary
pedagogy	tactile	coalesced	kinesthetic	relish

1. **Judge Decides Defendant's Former Marriage _____ to Current Accusation**

2. **Mayor Declares She Will _____ Rejuvenating Decaying Downtown Shopping Area**

3. *Management's and Labor's Goals _____ At Last Night's Negotiation Meeting*

4. **_____ Studies Enjoy Renewed Interest with College Students**

5. **Government Study Advocates More _____ Activities to Keep Kids Fit**

6. Local Students Quickly _____ to New Surroundings Days After Fire Destroys Their School

7. *Teachers From Across the Nation Gather for Weekend Conference on _____ and Technology*

8. New _____ Display at Children's Museum Lets Kids Feel River and Ocean Elements

9. *Latest _____ in City Hall Renovation Plans Show Swimming Pool Replacing Parking Lot*

10. Critics Demand Clearer Standards: Call Awards Process for Public Art Funds Too _____

3 Finish the story using the vocabulary words. Use each word once.

VOCABULARY LIST

coalesced	kinesthetic	permutations	subjective	interdisciplinary
assimilate	germane	pedagogy	relished	tactile

The History Project

My history instructor assigned us a(n) <u>(1)</u>_____ project. We had to connect history to at least one other field and make our presentation <u>(2)</u>_____ to either slavery or the Depression. Except for those limits we were free to create whatever we wanted. At first I thought

of doing a(n) <u>(3)</u>_____ project that involved showing the movements of the slaves in the fields. After several <u>(4)</u>_____, I decided to connect psychology with history. I would do a(n) <u>(5)</u>_____ presentation where my classmates could feel objects from the Depression to better understand the mind-set of the time. My various ideas (6)_____ in the middle of the night when I had a dream about sticking my hand into a sack and withdrawing a pile of dust. I worked hard to (7)_____ as much as I could about the Depression into my project.

I knew the evaluation of this project was going to have to be quite (8)_____ because it seemed impossible to have a right or wrong answer, as long as one stayed on topic. I liked my instructor's (9)_____ because it got me thinking about American history in creative ways. I (10)_____ the chance to show the class what I had learned about the Depression and to do it in an exciting way.

▌▌▌ INTERACTIVE EXERCISE

For each word give an example of how it could apply to a situation in college.

EXAMPLES: tactile   carrying ten books home from the library
            permutation   an addition to the science building

1. tactile   _____
2. kinesthetic   _____
3. germane   _____
4. interdisciplinary _____
5. subjective   _____
6. assimilate   _____
7. coalesce   _____
8. pedagogy   _____
9. permutation   _____
10. relish   _____

29 Computers

Technology Today

MATT: Thanks for talking to me, Dan; I am a computer **neophyte** and have so many questions about using the Internet. I'm afraid of committing some horrid **transgression** as I explore the Web. I hope I don't sound like an idiot. I had computerphobia for a long time, but computers have become so **ubiquitous**, I think I had better get used to them.

5 **DAN:** Don't worry. In computer **jargon** you're a newbie, and everyone's been a beginner at some point. I'll be happy to help : -). Let me go over a few **netiquette** points. When you are chatting, it is considered rude to **flame** people or make an angry or insulting remark. Writing in all capital letters looks like you are shouting and can be taken as flaming.

MATT: Thanks for the tip. I may have done that by accident. What does : -) mean after the word
10 "help"?

DAN: That is an **emoticon**, also known as a smiley. That one is a happy face. People use them to show their feelings. If I was sad, I might have written : - (.

MATT: Thanks : -) . If I want to use the Internet to find out about a particular subject, what should I do?

15 **DAN:** You can start by typing your interest and the word "**newsgroup**," such as "tennis news-group," into an Internet search engine like Yahoo! or Google, and you'll find a list of sites to check out. You can then join one of these newsgroups, which is just an online discussion group on a specific topic. When you first enter a discussion, take the time to read the Frequently Asked Question (FAQs) section and do some lurking so that you don't ask
20 questions that are likely to annoy the established users.

MATT: What is lurking?

DAN: Lurking is observing without participating. When you get a feel for a group, join in.

MATT: Are things I write on the Internet safe? Can anyone read my e-mail?

DAN: That depends on where you are posting material. If you are in a public discussion group,
25 people can read what you write. It is still uncertain who may have access to your e-mail. Although **encryption** has gotten better in recent years, especially as people send credit card information over the Internet, it is still a good idea to be cautious about the messages you write.

MATT: There is so much to learn. Do you think I will ever know it all?

30 **DAN:** I don't think anyone can. When the **prototype** for the modern computer was invented in the late 1940s, I don't think people really foresaw how many uses the computer would have. New words are coined daily in the computer field. Acronyms are especially impor-tant. In fact, I'll brb.

MATT: What does "brb" mean?
35 **MATT:** Dan, where are you?

▌▌▌ PREDICTING

Cover the Word List below as you do the Predicting exercise. For each set, write the definition on the line next to the word to which it belongs. If you are unsure, return to the reading on page 147, and underline any context clues you find. After you've made your predictions, uncover the Word List and check your answers. Place a checkmark in the boxes next to the words whose definitions you missed. These are the words you'll want to study closely.

SET ONE

online manners   violation of a law   or command   beginner   existing everywhere
the language of a particular profession or group

❑   1. **neophyte** (line 1) _____

❑   2. **transgression** (line 2) _____

❑   3. **ubiquitous** (line 4) _____

❑   4. **jargon** (line 5) _____

❑   5. **netiquette** (line 6) _____

SET TWO

an online discussion group   the model on which something is based   an online graphic
to insult or criticize online   a way of coding information

❑   6. **flame** (line 7) _____

❑   7. **emoticon** (line 11) _____

❑   8. **newsgroup** (line 15) _____

❑   9. **encryption** (line 26) _____

❑ 10. **prototype** (line 30) _____

▌▌▌ WORD LIST

emoticon
[i mō′ ti kon′]
n. a graphic made by combining punctuation marks and other characters to show one's feelings online

encryption
[en krip′ shən]
n. a way of coding information in a file or e-mail message so that if it is intercepted as it travels over a network, it cannot be read

flame
[flām]
v. 1. to insult or criticize angrily online
2. to behave in an offensive manner online; to rant
n. an act of angry criticism online

jargon
[jär′ gən, -gon]
n. 1. the language of a particular profession or group
2. unintelligible talk
3. pretentious language

neophyte
[nē′ ə fīt′]
n. a beginner or novice

netiquette
[net′ i kit, -ket′]
n. online manners or etiquette; an informal code of conduct for online behavior

newsgroup
[nooz′ groop′]
n. an online discussion group on a specific topic

prototype
[prō′ tə tīp′]
n. 1. the model on which something is based; a pattern
2. something that serves as a typical example of a group

transgression
[trans gresh′ ən, tranz-]
n. violation of a law, duty, or command; the exceeding of limits

ubiquitous
[yoo bik′ wi təs]
adj. existing or being everywhere, especially at the same time

1 Circle the correct meaning of each vocabulary word.

1. flame: to insult online   to compliment online

2. neophyte: expert   beginner

3. transgression: doing as commanded   violation of a law

4. jargon: pretentious language   simple language

5. ubiquitous: existing everywhere   found nowhere

6. netiquette: bad habits   online manners

7. prototype: a model   a silly example

8. encryption: coding information   sharing information

9. newsgroup: online discussion group   a weekly newsmagazine

10. emoticon: a word used to express   a graphic that shows one's feelings
    an opinion

2 Match each vocabulary word to the appropriate situation or example. Use each word once.

VOCABULARY LIST

neophyte	netiquette	encryption	prototype	flame
jargon	emoticon	newsgroup	transgression	ubiquitous

1. ; -) (winking)   _____

2. hard drive, software, CD-ROM, lol   _____

3. YOU'RE SO STUPID; TEN PEOPLE ALREADY
   ASKED THAT QUESTION   _____

4. .com   _____

5. the first washing machine   _____

6. on elementary education, on cars   _____

7. unsure which button to push to minimize a program   _____

8. reading the Frequently Asked Questions before you enter a discussion   _____

9. posting your friend's secret on the Internet   _____

10. #jf4^)6*9j   _____

3 Complete the following sentences using the vocabulary words. Use each word once.

1. I am a(n) _____ compared to my best friend who has been using computers for the last fifteen years.

2. To show my shock at Laura's e-mail announcement of her pregnancy, I used the _____ : - O.

3. I know it is considered rude, but I couldn't stop from _____ the person who kept making comments that were off-topic.

4. Now that I have been going to chat rooms for a few months, I understand how important _____ is. Just as in real life, there are rules to follow that make conversations run smoothly.

5. So much Internet _____ is based on acronyms that I'm often unsure of what someone is telling me.

6. Johnny committed a major _____ when he ate in front of the computer. He spilled cookie crumbs on the keyboard and got in trouble.

7. I was afraid to buy anything online because I thought my credit card number would be stolen, but I read about the _____ methods on a couple sites, and I have been successfully shopping electronically for months.

8. Computer terms have become so _____ that my five-year-old said he wanted an "e-hug" from me instead of a real hug.

9. The computer show featured a(n) _____ for a new computer that looked like a pencil.

10. After Ina's trip to Egypt, she joined a(n) _____ on archeology. She was really excited about sharing information on mummies and pyramids.

HINT

Make Learning Fun and Meaningful

Think about the kinds of activities you like to do, and then try to incorporate the qualities involved in those activities into your learning experiences. If you like group activities (team sports, going to big parties), create study groups. If you like to draw, add visual elements to your notes, draw what happens in a story you read, or make a diagram to help you understand a concept. If you like to write, create stories or poems related to your studies or keep a journal about your learning. The more you enjoy what you do, whether in school or at work, the more you want to do it. Take the time to find ways to make your life and learning fun.

▌▌▐▌ INTERACTIVE EXERCISE

Pretend you have joined a newsgroup on a subject that interests you, and write three postings using at least six of the vocabulary words.

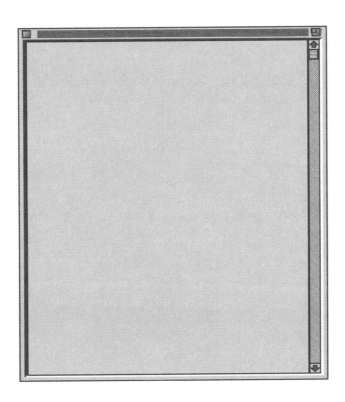

Focus on Chapters 21–29

1. _____

2. _____

3. _____

4. _____

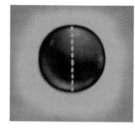

5. _____

6. _____

7. _____

8. _____

9. _____

10. _____

11. _____

12. _____

The following activities give you a chance to interact some more with the vocabulary words you've been learning. By looking at art, acting, writing, taking tests, and doing a crossword puzzle, you will see which words you know well and which you still need to work with.

▌▐▌▌ ART

Match each picture on page 152 to one of the following vocabulary words. Use each word once.

VOCABULARY LIST

eponym	toponym	perennial	emoticon
oust	facet	kinesthetic	triumvirate
ominous	bisect	amulet	symmetrical

▌▐▌▌ DRAMA

Charades: You will be given one of the following words to act out in class. Think about how this word could be demonstrated without speaking. The other people in class will try to guess what word you are showing.

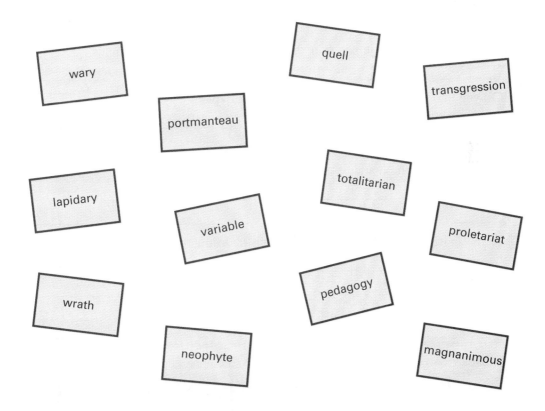

Answer the following questions to further test your understanding of the vocabulary words.

1. What type of interdisciplinary class would you like to take?

   _____

   _____

2. Name a quality that would be essential in a utopian society.

   _____

   _____

3. Name a field that uses a lot of statistics.

   _____

   _____

4. List two kinds of decisions people frequently oscillate about.

   _____   _____

5. Name two newsgroups you would be interested in joining.

   _____   _____

6. Name a belief or idea you are immutable about.

   _____

   _____

7. Give two examples of jargon from the medical, legal, or computer fields.

   _____   _____

8. Do you find studying etymologies interesting? Explain why or why not.

   _____

   _____

9. Name a job people should be meticulous in doing.

   _____

   _____

10. Name an item that is supposedly impervious to destruction.

    _____

    _____

11. Give two examples of things that can be malignant.

    _____   _____

12. What are two items you would want to buy from a bona fide maker instead of on the street?

    _____   _____

1 Finish the story using the vocabulary words. Use each word once.

VOCABULARY LIST

archaic	finite	germane	milieu	qualms
attribute	gamut	inherent	paranoid	ubiquitous
enigma	garner			

The Awards Banquet

We thought our college was going to ___(1)_____ several awards at the Statewide Recognition Ceremony. The categories we had entered ran the ___(2)_____ from the arts to the sciences. The ___(3)_____ in the banquet hall was sophistication combined with fear. Everyone was trying to

look relaxed and confident, but it was easy to tell that everyone was nervous. I suppose anxiety is ___(4)_____ in any awards event. Smiles, handshakes, and shouts of "good luck" were ___(5)_____. Everywhere I turned someone was congratulating me for just being there. After a few minutes, I just wanted to get the night over with. There is only a(n) ___(6)_____ amount of insincerity that I can handle.

We were served dinner, and then the awards began. The prize for Best Literary Magazine went to Newark College. I didn't understand how that could be. The magazines entered in the competition were supposed to focus on the subject of literacy. There was no way that the articles in their magazine could have been considered ___(7)_____ to that topic. Of all the colleges entered, I was sure they were going to lose most of all. The next award was for Best Dramatic Production. Eastern College won for *The Old Plank Road*. The reviews of that show were horrid. What ___(8)_____ system were the judges using in making their choices? The following award was my category: Best Business Plan. Our team had developed a plan that had saved our local bank thousands of dollars and increased customer satisfaction. I didn't have any ___(9)_____ about our winning. When they announced that Montana College had won, I practically fell off my chair. It was an absolute ___(10)_____ as to what the judges wanted. I had seen Montana's plan; it could have been written by first graders. We went home empty-handed. I didn't know what to <u>(11)</u>_____ our losses to. All the winners had seemed like sure losers. I was feeling a bit <u>(12)</u>_____. Maybe our college had somehow offended the judges. We were certainly going to have to do something different to win next year.

2 Pick the word that best completes each sentence.

1. Emily and Becky finally decided it was a matter of _____ as to whether the movie was good. Their definitions of "good" were not the same.

   a. emoticons   b. intervals   c. semantics   d. permutations

2. The kids enjoyed the _____ exhibit at the museum. They enjoyed touching all the animal hides.

   a. tactile   b. ubiquitous   c. inherent   d. finite

3. Milt found that the _____ of working at the doughnut shop faded after he'd eaten the first two dozen doughnuts.

   a. jargon   b. amulet   c. gradation   d. luster

4. I thought it was a _____ that people need eight hours of sleep each night, but when I fell asleep in my soup, I realized I couldn't get by on two hours of sleep for long.

   a. neologism   b. fallacy   c. triumvirate   d. dementia

5. When Alexander started taking lessons, his skill at the piano _____.

   a. burgeoned   b. flamed   c. relished   d. quelled

6. Because our government is a _____, it is important that everyone votes.

   a. newsgroup   b. pedagogy   c. republic   d. vestige

7. The plans for the party _____ at the last minute, and everything turned out beautifully.

   a. coined   b. ousted   c. bisected   d. coalesced

8. Phil isn't familiar with many _____ related to computers. He was really worried when I told him that I had to buy a new mouse for my computer.

   a. underpinnings   b. neologisms   c. statistics   d. qualms

9. I thought it was _____ of Joan not to invite me to her party, but my mother said it wasn't such a big deal.

   a. archaic   b. heinous   c. utopian   d. impervious

10. _____ has become so important to communication today; I don't think people would use the Internet so much unless they were assured of some privacy.

    a. ellipsis   b. enigma   c. eponym   d. encryption

11. I was scared when the doctor told me that a _____ in my lungs was keeping me from breathing correctly.

    a. toponym   b. neologism   c. dysfunction   d. facet

12. At first the hole in the wall seemed _____, but when Skippy squeezed under it and ran away, we regretted ignoring it.

    a. utopian   b. inconsequential   c. inherent   d. finite

CROSSWORD PUZZLE

Use the following words to complete the crossword puzzle. You will use each word once.

VOCABULARY LIST

assimilate	netiquette
bourgeoisie	permutation
coin	placebo
dementia	prototype
ellipsis	quota
epicene	relish
flame	subjective
gradation	underpinning
interval	vestige
manifest	viable

Across

3. a foundation
4. a change through stages
9. an omission
12. capable of living
16. a slight amount
17. a pause
18. the number permitted
19. online manners
20. to invent

Down

1. the middle class
2. the model on which something is based
5. madness
6. SHUT UP
7. transformation
8. to absorb
10. existing in the mind
11. evident
13. belonging to both sexes
14. without any real medicinal value
15. Oh, that's good!

ANALOGIES APPENDIX

An **analogy** shows a relationship between words. Working with analogies helps you see connections between words, which is a crucial critical thinking skill. Analogies are written as follows: big : large :: fast : quick. The colon (:) means "is to." The analogy reads, "big *is to* large as fast *is to* quick." To complete analogies simply find a relationship between the first pair of words and then look for a similar relationship in another pair of words. In the example above, *big* and *large* are synonyms and so are *fast* and *quick*.

Common relationships used in analogies are synonyms, antonyms, examples, part to a whole, grammatical structure, cause and effect, sequences, and an object to a user or to its use.

The analogies in this book come in matching and fill-in-the-blank forms. Try the following analogies for practice.

Matching

1. old : young :: _____   a. preface : book

2. clip coupons : go shopping:: _____   b. put on shoes : take a walk

3. peel : banana :: _____   c. low wages : strike

4. no rain : drought :: _____   d. rested : tired

Fill-in-the-Blank

writer	passion	abduct	sadly

5. frozen : chilled :: kidnap : _____

6. interrupting : rude :: embracing : _____

7. slow : slowly :: sad : _____

8. baton : conductor :: computer : _____

Answers

1. d   [antonyms]
2. b   [sequence]
3. a   [part to a whole]
4. c   [cause and effect]
5. abduct   [synonyms]
6. passion   [an example]
7. sadly   [grammatical structure]
8. writer   [object to user]

CREATE YOUR OWN FLASH CARDS

Using flash cards can be an immensely helpful way to study vocabulary words. The process of making the flash cards will aid you in remembering the meanings of the words. Index cards work well as flash cards or you may use the following pages of flash card templates to get you started. Put the word and the pronunciation on the front of the card. Elements you may want to include on the back of the card will vary according to the word and your preferred learning style. Consider the ideas below and find what works best for you.

1. **The part of speech:** Write an abbreviation for the part of speech, such as *n.* for noun or *v.* for verb. This addition will help when you are writing sentences.
2. **A simple definition:** Use the definitions in the book or modify them to something that has meaning for you. Use a definition you can remember.
3. **A sentence:** Make up your own sentence that correctly uses the word. Try to use a context clue to help you remember the word. It might help to put yourself or friends in the sentences to personalize your use of the word. If you really like a sentence from the book, you can use that too.
4. **A drawing:** If you are a visual learner, try drawing the word. Some words especially lend themselves to this method. Your drawing doesn't have to be fancy; it should just help you remember the meaning of the word.
5. **A mnemonic device:** These are methods to help your memory. They can be rhymes, formulas, or clues. For example: Stationery with an *e* is the kind that goes in an *e*nvelope. Make up any connections you can between the word and its meaning.
6. **Highlight word parts:** Circle one or more word parts (prefixes, roots, or suffixes) that appear in the word and write the meaning(s) next to the word part: for example, in(duc)e. See the Word Parts chapters in the text for more on word parts. ↳ *to lead*

Whatever you do, make the cards personally meaningful. Find the techniques that work for you and use them in creating your cards. Then make the time to study the cards. Carry them with you and study them any chance you get. Also, find someone who will be tough in quizzing you with the cards. Have the person hold up a card, and you give the meaning and use the word in a sentence. Don't quit until you are confident that you know what each word means.

Sample card

Front	Back
audible [ô də bəl]	*adj. loud enough to hear* Even though she was whispering, Liz's comments were audible across the room.

WORD LIST